About the Author

English born Author, Carole Ferch-Johnson grew up in Northern Ireland. During her high school years, she immigrated to Australia. She continued her education in the United States with a BA in German and an MA in Pastoral Psychology and Counselling. The latter equipped her for a career in people helping. Ultimately, she was appointed an advocate and supporter of women in pastoral ministry and completed a PhD in New Testament studies in her senior years. Drawing on what she has learned from others, it is her life experience that has given rise to this book.

LIVING PATCHWORK:
Lessons Learned from Life

Carole Ferch-Johnson PhD

LIVING PATCHWORK:
Lessons Learned from Life

Olympia Publishers
London

www.olympiapublishers.com
OLYMPIA PAPERBACK EDITION

Copyright © Carole Ferch-Johnson PhD 2023

The right of Carole Ferch-Johnson PhD to be identified as author of this work has been asserted in accordance with sections 77 and 78 of the Copyright, Designs and Patents Act 1988.

All Rights Reserved

No reproduction, copy or transmission of this publication may be made without written permission.
No paragraph of this publication may be reproduced, copied or transmitted save with the written permission of the publisher, or in accordance with the provisions of the Copyright Act 1956 (as amended).

Any person who commits any unauthorised act in relation to this publication may be liable to criminal prosecution and civil claims for damage.

A CIP catalogue record for this title is available from the British Library.

ISBN: 978-1-80439-396-3

This is a work of fiction.
Names, characters, places and incidents originate from the writer's imagination. Any resemblance to actual persons, living or dead, is purely coincidental.

First Published in 2023

Olympia Publishers
Tallis House
2 Tallis Street
London
EC4Y 0AB

Printed in Great Britain

Dedication

To my sons who taught me to know the other half of life.

Prologue

Close to tears with frustration, I flung my puckered sewing with angry force and landed it on a distant corner of the living room floor. I had toiled at stitching for several hours with the sewing machine my father had bought. Dad had been pleased with my exam results since they had qualified me for six years' education in a private grammar school at government expense. Consequently, he had rewarded my efforts with the gift of this machine. I had wanted it for some time because I had watched my seamstress aunt who lived with us. On her sewing machine, she had plied her well-honed skills with enviable success, and I had said I would like to own one too. Try as I might, however, I did not have my aunt's artistic touch, nor could 1 produce her quality of work. So, with my energies expended on the throw, I declared aloud,

'I really wanted to make a patchwork quilt of crazy design with all these scraps of material but I think that goal is quite beyond my reach.' Seated by the warm coal fire, Mum looked up from her knitting and nodded her assent.

'That's right,' she sniffed. 'You're a girl after my own heart. I never could sew anything either.' Hearing her remark, I swung round on my chair and faced her—our eyes locked in amused accord. Was that a challenge I detected in her candid comment? Was she testing my reaction with her frank words and wry smile? Whether or not she meant it to happen, I sensed a contest coming on between the sewing assignment and me. It was fraught with a strong determination that welled up from somewhere deep inside me and spilled out with wilful force onto the errant quilt. Whether my mother's challenge was real or imagined, my drive to finish what I had started surged forth and urged me towards the source of my vexation. I would retrieve the crumpled quilt from the corner where it lay. I advanced towards it and, snatching it up, vowed to complete the task come what may. I was bent on beating the thing that had threatened me with defeat and I would make a decent piece of handiwork of it or die in the attempt!

The patchwork quilt was to be my entry in a local competition where a group of girls, my age, planned to enter their work. Having grown up together till we had reached thirteen, we had formed natural friendships and taken them for granted. It was a case of everyone knowing everyone else in the village. Ours was a closely knit community where a number of Protestant churches clustered about the village 'green'. There was a time when the green had boasted several oak trees with limes and elms planted between, and a soft daisied grass had carpeted the ground. Decades had passed since then and by the time our childish feet had begun to tramp the green, its grassy surface had given way to a hardy tarmacadam. The green still hosted a few trees as tokens of its emerald days and though there was little left underfoot that could be called green any longer, it continued to be known by its original name. As for our handiwork, we were to display it on trestles set up on the village green and one from amongst the entries would be judged the winner. The work should be neat and skilful, whilst the thing created must be practically useful.

Our village was nestled in County Down, home to the fertile fields, parochial towns and charming hamlets of Northern Ireland's southeast corner. Evident to the eye from any moderate elevation, more than anything else the local landscape resembled crazy patchwork. Small, variegated fields of grain, potato, turnip, cabbage and pasture made up the rural design. The fields were hedged about with stone walls. These formed a foundation hidden from view by the sturdy growth of the prickly hawthorn shrub. Passing near the front door of the little cottage we called home, was a mile-long road that ran from a nearby farm to the village centre. The road was narrow, though sealed with tarmacadam, and on each side tender greenery and delicate flowers caressed its brittle edges. Towards the end of winter when the transient snowfall had all but melted away, snowdrops would appear—the earliest wildflowers to deck the roadside verges. These were followed soon by an abundance of yellow petals: some primrose; some cowslip and the rest the common buttercup. In summer, banks of purple wild sweet pea rose up from the ditch beyond the verge and met the roots of the fragrant honeysuckle and dog rose. These stretched upwards to their full height and were supported by the hedgerow looming above. As the road rose past our cottage to form a gentle hill, it was flanked by bushes of gorse and broom flaunting their golden blossom in bright display. These filled the air with perfume as they vied for the attention of any passing bee. Further along, banks of earth mounted up on each side of the road and, covered with bracken fern, fell steeply away to the fields below. On one side of the road, the mound rolled in modest descent to a large field of blue green corn where, here and there, the scarlet head of a showy poppy nodded above the growing grain in brilliant array. On the other side of the road, the bank sank down to a sea of clustered bluebells bobbing and swaying beneath the spreading foliage of a giant sycamore tree. In autumn, village children ambled along the road as they wandered home from school. Tempted to gather the ripened berries that hung in clusters on beckoning brambles, they braved the bed of stinging nettles to reach and harvest the soft ripe fruit. Then the tell-tale juice ran down their dimpled chins in purple rivulets and smeared their chubby cheeks with sticky sweetness. When the nettles caught their small bare legs and left a fiery welt, the children grabbed at the nearby dock-leaf and soothed away the angry sting with a firm medicinal rub. For me, this was the road much travelled because it led to everywhere known to my young life and especially to the village centre and its green.

The village belonged to a part of the world where Scottish heritage and a frugal mentality were cultural realities. So the organisers of the day had offered no surprise when they pronounced the theme of our girlhood competition 'A demonstration of thrift.' The exhibit judged to best embody this highly valued virtue would win its entrant a simple award. Though the winner would earn high acclaim, in keeping with the theme of thrift the award itself would be a modest token. It would be a simple metal badge fastened to the winner's cardigan and worn with pride. The award would last until its paint rubbed off or its pin rusted through. These signs of deterioration would take up to a year and by then, there would be a further competition and another winner to claim a new award. Alas, on the day of my sewing disaster, my planned entry to the competition was far from fit to achieve any acclaim. Chagrined at the difference between aspiration and accomplishment, I examined the results of my efforts once again. Was there any hope for this symbol of industry and frugality? I wondered. Could anyone—could I—redeem it and make it what it was meant to be? With a valiant effort at finding a modicum of patience and a good deal of grit, I straightened out the crushed beginnings of my planned exhibit and looked it over carefully.

Up to this point, I had been intent on sewing together some mismatched remnants of cloth to enable thrift to take on tangible form in the shape of a usable quilt. Now, however, I began to examine the scraps of material with new eyes to discover their individual features and to work out how they could best be joined in one continuous whole. Dismay grew as my awareness of the disparity amongst the scraps increased. I saw how widely they differed from one another in texture, weight, colour and design. How could rich red velvet co-exist with purple satin or a cluster of springy wool checks sit well with soft blue voile? If only the scraps could be more homogeneous and not so incompatible, maybe they could combine. The problem was, they were the only remnants of cloth I had, and the patchwork would have to be created from them or not at all.

As I considered this, I saw that maybe the random scraps could fit together with interest, even fascination, if not obvious beauty. In this they began to take on a different meaning altogether from the practical task I believed was mine. Though I did not fully understand it at the time, the exhibit in its ultimate form was to be much more than a symbol of thrift formed by the inexperienced hands of a teenage girl. It would become a more subtle symbol of the whole of life with its hard rough patches and soft smooth pieces and it would take a lifetime to create. Like Alfred Lord Tennyson's Lady of Shallot who wove her eternal tapestry, I was destined to daily develop my crazy patchwork while ever I drew breath. It would become an expression of my whole life with its enduring and passing qualities, its beautiful and ugly parts, its elegant and common scraps, its warm and cool inclusions and its darker and lighter hues. It would become the work of a life's experiences: some good and some bad; some welcome and some unwanted but all present to take their place in the completed work—in the complexity known as life. Would it result in a neat and skilful finish or would there be aspects to regret?

This realisation told me that whether I wished it or not, I would spend the rest of my life creating a living patchwork and hoping it would come together with more success than failure. I would not be alone in this venture, however. There would be millions of people who recognise they too have a bundle of diverse scraps from which to fashion a life. In its unlimited modes of expression living patchwork would yield for them as many variations as there are designs to be had. This would ensure individuality and uniqueness with no two lives lived in exactly the same way. The samples of patchwork they would create would differ widely from each other just as one life differs from another. The results would produce countless varieties depicting years of hard-won gains and painful losses; days of joy and nights of grief; wonderful surprises and bitter disappointments. The only person qualified to interpret the various patches, their quality and kind and to understand how they come together to form the whole is the one who lives the life.

In the following chapters, I will tell the story of living patchwork. It will be my own unique story made up of the realities of life including lessons I have learned from living it. In the telling, I will touch on the lives of many others and will show how life, though a crazy patchwork, can be lived to its fullest and best. In these pages mistakes are made, problems confronted but not always solved, and difficulties overcome. Therefore it is a true story, but for their protection, the names of people are fictitious. Life lends itself to the use of metaphor in an effort to grasp the meaning of its course. Perhaps the metaphor of crazy patchwork with its chaos and design, its many varieties of materials and its eventual emergence as an acceptable piece of art might be included as one of them. Whether the telling of my story is simply a prosaic collection of the ordinary to be found in anyone's day-to-day life or holds some interest and enough insight to make it worth the writing is for you, dear reader, to decide.

Chapter 1

To Be or not to Be

It was touch and go whether I would arrive or not. Then, on a chilly April day, gravity pulled my long slender body, naked and wet, into England's County Kent and I was officially born. In pathetic defiance of my mother's will, and determined to make an entrance, whether I was wanted or not, I announced my coming into the world with six convulsive sneezes. I think they must have counted for something for ill-prepared as she was, my mother was moved by them to bear up bravely and accept the fact that she was now a parent.

In some measure, Mum's ambivalence towards motherhood was understandable. When she was a child herself, necessity had demanded she stay home from school to care for several younger siblings. This allowed her single-parent mother of seven to work at a full-time job in order to support the family. These circumstances, however, had deprived my mother of all but the basic rudiments of an education and driven her to the firm decision that she would avoid producing children of her own.

As though peering out through the invisible bars of a prison cell, she had declared to no one in particular, 'I've served my time caring for someone else's offspring and I want none of my own.' It was an honest protest and sincerely meant, but it did not last. My presence, with all its newborn needs, soon transformed her assumed indifference into a strong protective love. This proved to be my emotional salvation for I was spared the bequest of her low self-worth with its resultant sense of inadequacy. As a consequence, I grew up contented and well-adjusted—convinced I could do anything I chose—albeit the only child of my devoted parents.

Precarious though my beginnings were, once born, I began to craft my crazy patchwork life as a child of emotional privilege. My first patch was undoubtedly smooth, soft textured and light toned. In living with it, I was off to a splendid start. Despite beginning my days in the midst of the Second World War, I was aware of none of its horror. Unconscious of the presence of conflict, I passed my earliest years peacefully nurtured on the familiar stretch of fabric where I first drew breath. Happily, I found it to be woven from strong strands of warm affection and durable threads of unfailing security. Although it was only the first scrap of material in my living patchwork, it was destined to lay down the firm foundation of essential resilience I would sorely need in times to come. But, would resilience be enough to help me endure the rough dark fragments to follow as they came to join the already present stuff of an easier life? The answer was that only time could tell just how rough and dark future pieces would turn out to be. It could not be known from the outset if all the resources enabling me to accept and meet these patches and to incorporate them into the fabric of life would really be available.

The first dark patch I remember was delivered to me when I was six years old. I was walking down an Irish country lane with my father when I spotted a dog, a Welsh corgi, standing motionless in the middle of the path. I had frequently visited Grandma's house where Trixie, her 'big dog on short legs,' was a resident pet. I was familiar with the corgi's patient ways for she was ever playfully at my heel. Together we walked and ran over grassy hills and through fields of hay. We romped and tumbled as one on mossy slopes and skipped our way across narrow streams. After a breathless frolic, Trixie would roll onto her back at my feet in final triumph with her legs stretched up in invitation. It was time for a vigorous belly rub while I carefully avoided the sweet spot that would irritate her and cause an involuntary kicking of her leg. My reward was to see her close her eyes and stretch out her neck in obvious canine pleasure. So, on spotting the Trixie look-alike, excitement grew and I let go my father's hand to race ahead and pat the corgi while I called to it in friendly tones: 'Hello, are you Trixie's sister? What's your name? Is it written on your collar?' As I came to within a yard of it, however, my joy melted away in disappointed bewilderment. The dog I was sure I had seen turned out to be quite inanimate.

'Oh no, It's only an empty cardboard box!' I moaned as my father caught up with me. 'I was sure it was a corgi, Dad.' My mistake confessed, I shrugged and laughed up into my father's face, but there was no mirth in his expression. The relaxed smile he normally wore had vanished. It was overcome by a look of unmistakable concern. Commonly a loquacious man, his normal burst of wordy affirmation was lost in an unfamiliar silence. Something was terribly wrong with my vision and he was recognising it for the very first time.

A few days later I returned to school and, early in the term, my standard one teacher held up a picture of a farmyard scene. I knew this because, in response to the teacher's promptings, the children around me were identifying the animals in the frame. I was puzzled as to how they could do this when there were no animals to be seen. Soon, however, a letter came from school addressed to my parents. It contained the chilling lines:

'Your child appears to have some difficulty seeing. She may need glasses. We recommend she be taken for eye testing.' 'Some difficulty' was a cautious understatement. The marker for normal vision is 20/20 but my test resulted in a score of less than 20/200 in both eyes. Here was a clear case of legal blindness and it was mine to own. Denial is our first defence against unwelcome news and my parents quickly resorted to it.

'Glasses will be the answer for sure,' they insisted. 'Lenses will fix the problem just like they do for everyone else with poor vision.' Upon much urging from every adult known to me, I wore glasses, though they were not the answer and they did not fix the problem. They simply could not. Eventually it would be discovered that I had a genetically transmitted condition that defied the attempt of any lens to correct. Ultimately my parents' persuasive talk of the benefits of spectacles and how well I would suit them ceased, and the fragile hope of improvement they had tried to hold out to me evaporated. In their eagerness to help, they had crossed the line between harsh reality and wishful thinking. Nonetheless, lens after lens had been tried in an effort to find the right one, but there was no right one. It simply had to be faced that no lens existed with the capacity to correct my vision. It was my optic nerve that was severely compromised and there was no remedy for that.

The fact was, my vision was not blurred but the fragmentary images I saw, though clear and sharp, resembled an incomplete jigsaw puzzle made up of minute pieces where most of them were missing. There was also a tell-tale pallor that characterised the optic discs at the back of my eyes. This was thought to be symptomatic of a severe optic nerve deficiency. Otherwise, to the casual observer and even to the examining professional, my eyes looked to be quite normal. My sharp-eyed Mum was devastated at the discovery, but I skipped happily out of the clinic and down the street holding her hand. I was quite oblivious to the fact that my mysterious condition would defy a definitive diagnosis for the next thirty years.

Thus, the dark shadowy shape of a large irregular piece was added to my crazy patchwork and was destined to affect every aspect of my life. It meant I was unable to read large print, even at a short distance, and I fell behind in blackboard dependent subjects at school. Out of doors, street names were unreadable and road signs undecipherable to me. More than once, crossing a road alone provided a life threatening hazard as I dodged contact with oncoming traffic and induced fear in many a driver. It was during these early school years that I found myself tramping along the same narrow country road I had walked with my father the day I had spotted the 'corgi' cardboard box. It was a cold November afternoon and darkness was closing in around me. Ahead was a copse of silver birch trees where the road cut through. As I walked between the ghostly trunks, their bare branches reaching high to the sky, a stranger rode swiftly towards me on a black Raleigh bike. He was wearing a charcoal suit and his cuffs were clamped to his ankles with a set of trouser clips. Pulling up in front of me he blocked my way and demanded,

'Aren't you afraid, little girl, to be walking alone on this empty road?' Being afraid had not crossed my mind so I answered truthfully,

'No.' Then with a flash of inspiration gathered from an unknown source, I continued, 'Besides, I'm not alone. I'm with Jesus and he's with me.' The man's face softened and creased into a pleasant smile.

'I'm glad to hear that,' he responded and pulling a picture card from the inside breast pocket of his jacket, he handed it to me.

'Here's a card to remind you of it,' he said. The card read: 'The Lord your God goes with you. He will never leave you nor forsake you' (Deut 31:6). I thanked the man and with a light-hearted skip continued on my homeward way. I was convinced that either behind me, or in front, and certainly nearby, Jesus was walking along the same twilit road.

Dark and pervasive though the patch of poor vision was, it was relieved by a lighter piece. This lay in the fact that I could do well in subjects that were less dependent on seeing the blackboard than they were on hearing words and memorising them.

'Where possible, listen and retain without the need to see,' became my unspoken policy from that time on. This strategy yielded the desired results when, along with the able pupils amongst my standard five peers, I managed to gain a government scholarship. This was of consequence for it paid for tuition and textbooks at a private grammar school and continued for the duration of my secondary education.

Despite my father's constant efforts to create a perfect childhood for me, the dark patch of my early life persisted beyond my years of innocence. It stretched to my days in high school and offered a formidable challenge when I confronted mathematics, geography and the sciences but could see little of the blackboard, the maps or the experiments associated with these subjects. In order to be of help, well-meaning teachers would seat me as close as possible to the item on display, but this was at a social cost for my fellow students complained volubly,

'We can't see past her, Sir,' or, 'Miss, does she have to sit there blocking our view?' From the first, I had been 'mainstreamed' in a government primary school rather than sent to a special establishment designed to cater to my visual disability. Consequently, I was subject to normal expectation and 'had a go' at whatever my fully sighted peers attempted. At times they bettered me in the process, and at times I bettered them. Challenging though it was, it was the best thing in the absence of over-protection or of a particular focus on my severe disability, I grew up perceiving myself to be normal and capable like any one of my peers and not as one set apart from them for a peculiar reason. The result was that during my school years, I was not particularly conscious that I had a disability. This was to change, however, as childhood gave way to girlhood and growth brought increased awareness. I was yet to learn just how awkward and undesirable this particular piece would become in my efforts at living patchwork.

Chapter 2

To Grow or not to Grow

As you would expect, the shade of my first dark patch deepened over time and its size increased as I grew. Still, a fuller realisation of my difference from others dawned rather slowly and only came to completion when I reached my teens. By then, the print in textbooks had grown smaller and more difficult to read. This made it increasingly easier to memorise facts and figures than to try to look them up. I also became conscious of how much more my friends could observe in the world around us and how much I must be missing. I noticed, too, how dependent I was on their verbal descriptions: from the prevalence of traffic on the roads we crossed to the makes and models of passing cars; from the identity of an approaching person to the characteristics of an animal or bird; from the colour of the blossom on a shrub or bush, to the size and shape of a garden flower.

It was this awareness that also helped me gain perspective on my chronic incompetence on the sports field. Try as I might, my performance was poor in any game involving a ball. During our primary school years, the invariable community sport of choice was a game of rounders. According to their assessment of our ability on the field, a class leader would select team members to play on their side against the other team. I had a virtual double in my class, Anna McNish. People often remarked on how alike we were, and occasionally confused us for one another. Both of us were tall and slim, fair haired and blue eyed with two stringy plaits protruding from behind our ears and only reaching to our shoulders. To complete the likeness, each of us wore a blue and white gingham dress for several days of the summer term and a green gym-frock in winter. There were some major differences between Anna and me as well. One was most obvious when teams were picked for rounders. Anna was always chosen first and I, last. There was no mystery to this for Anna was a champion with the ball. She had deceptively thin arms but they were made of high tensile steel and when she strode onto the pitch, the opposing team would gasp. Then they would fan out and step back several paces in a vain effort to catch the small leather ball as it torpedoed off her wooden bat.

'Watch out!' the captain of the other team would cry, 'McNish is on to bat!' One day I played on the opposite team to Anna. I was positioned as far outfield as it was possible to be when Anna hit the ball. The next thing I knew, a searing pain was shooting through my right shoulder as the ball made contact with my collarbone.

'Catch it, catch it!' bawled my team-mates as I lay sprawled on the grass with the little hard sphere innocuously resting at my side. Amidst the groans of disapproval from my own team, sweet-natured Anna, full of compassion and apology, came jogging down from fourth base to where I lay. Gingerly, she helped me to my feet and dusted me down—worried she might have caused me serious harm. But for me, it was just another day at the mercy of my nemesis, the ball.

Nor did my relationship with balls improve as I stepped reluctantly onto the high school sports arena. Hockey mistress, Jean McLeod was on the field. She was a pretty pigeon-toed woman in her early thirties with a gift for making a poorly performing girl feel small. With a sharp blast on her over-shrill whistle, she signalled to me and directed,

'Come over here and we'll try you out for centre forward.' As a position of prestige in the team, this was it. After the bully off, however, the ball was nowhere to be seen and the little centre forward on the opposite side was jumping around on one foot and howling with pain. Apparently, I had inadvertently whacked her unseen fingers with my stick while the ball had dribbled away and was lurking somewhere behind me. The high popularity rating I had been cultivating sank that day to an all-time low and it took weeks of hard work to claw some of it back. In this instance, it did not help to go home seeking solace from Mum. In her youth she had played centre forward for Belfast's first eleven and, in response to my bid for sympathy, rolled her eyes and tutted with impatience—somewhat reminiscent of Jean McLeod.

Water sports featured low on the favourites list for most of our village girls, even in summer. But I had a fearless friend in my next door neighbour, Donna. She brought a sizeable piece of colourful fabric to include in my living patchwork.

Like me, she loved to run across the open fields, 'To outstrip the bulls,' she claimed and to hang upside down from farm gates. She happily hopped over rustic stiles, vaulted fences and jumped across gurgling streams. Because water held a magnetic attraction for both of us, it only took the merest word like,

'Let's go and jump rivers,' from one of us and we were off on our bikes heading for the nearby farm. I must admit, when it came to courage I had my limitations but Donna did not seem to share them. She was two years younger than I and a good deal smaller. Still, she made up for her lack of stature with a high degree of common sense, practical wisdom and a first rate spirit of adventure. Of course, river jumping was never complete unless we 'fell in' so our jaunts usually ended with two pairs of sodden socks and shoes. On one occasion it had rained a lot and the stream we frequented was wider and deeper than usual. This meant that 'falling in' amounted to a full body soak for anyone who could not quite reach, or could not quite see, the opposite bank. Donna's vision was undiminished, so she quickly estimated the distance she needed to jump, and sprang with alacrity, landing firmly on solid ground.

'Come on, it's easy!' she prompted, 'You can do it, no problem.' Tense with anticipation I placed one foot forward and rocked back and forth in a bid to gather momentum. Leaping high I cleared the brook, but descended on a deceptive tuft of weed that overhung the water. The plant gave way under my weight and I took the plunge. When the shock had worn off, I found myself submerged to the neck and reclining on the bed of the cold brown stream. Despite the fact it was summer, the cool climate of County Down was not conducive to remaining wet for very long and, once recovered from her un-suppressible giggles, Donna had the solution.

'Let's dispense with your wet things. We will pack them away in the front basket of your bike. Then we can share my dry clothes. You can wear my linen dress and ride home barefoot while I keep my cotton petticoat and cardigan,' she offered. When I pulled it over my head, her linen dress proved much too short for the modesty standards of the 1950s. Nonetheless, I agreed the level of decency we had achieved would have to do for the time being and we peddled home with all speed. On our arrival, Donna's mother was horrified at the sight of us, but mine just stifled a grin at the news of our escapade. After all, as a girl, had she not taught her siblings how to pole vault on a broomstick over the rivers and streams that criss-crossed the Bog Meadows of

West Belfast? And had she not narrowly missed a singeing in a large street bonfire by skirting its outer edge on her bike while her less nimble sister had ridden, out of control, through its middle? These are evidence that the primeval attraction of water and fire still drew the women who shared my genes into tricky situations.

Whether it was compensation for my disability or simple over-confidence I am not sure, but water was nearly my undoing. One bright sunny day an annual excursion took six of us girls to the seaside. On the beach of a docile bay, five wooden boats stood waiting for hire with their watchful keeper alert to the prospect of profiting from them.

'Come on,' I urged, 'let's hop in and go for a row.' Serious minded Sheila was dubious, 'Can you row?' she demanded. Well, I had seen my father row and it had not looked difficult so I replied, 'Oh yes, no problem.' At the time, little crafts like these were not equipped with life-vests and it did not occur to me that I might be the only one in the group able to swim. So we set off, packed tightly together in the small vessel where I seated myself between the oars. To set us off, the boat-keeper gave us a robust push and I began to pull. It was not difficult to get out into the middle of the bay, and despite my erratic efforts, the little boat seemed happy enough to stay on course. I beamed with pleasure at the approving nods of my friends who were noting my obvious skill. As it happens, sunny weather in County Down was never very dependable and soon the blue sky covered over with dark grey cloud and it began to rain.

'Let's get back,' ordered Sheila.

'Yes, let's go back!' chorused the other four. I was soon to discover, however, that while rowing out was one thing, getting back in was quite another. The once compliant little boat suddenly developed a mind of its own and, despite my tugging on the oars it flatly refused to move towards land. Preferring to rotate in playful circles it was totally unconscious of our anxious concern. While I struggled and my friends complained;, it took about thirty minutes for the rain to soak us through. Meanwhile, the boat-keeper seeing our predicament sped out in a motorboat to rescue us from the deep. To add to our problems, the warm woollen coats we were wearing were in no way waterproof. Once wet, they clung to us with heavy, cumbersome tenacity helping the rising wind to chill us to the bone. Finally, arriving numb to the core from the cold and stiff with indignation, my five bedraggled friends clambered ashore in their soggy garb and marched up the beach in high dudgeon. This time, there was no ball in play for me to blame. The fault lay in my having too high a measure of self-confidence in addition to too low a degree of skill, and poor eyesight did not even feature. With my standing in the eyes of my friends considerably diminished once again, I was thankful for their eventual willingness to forgive. Thus the strong bond of friendship that held us together overcame the potential damage to our relationship making it reasonably short lived.

When it came to swimming or diving into water, I stood in the shadow of my mother. Her athletic prowess was well-known and she was determined I would learn from her. So, held up by the straps on the back of my 'bathing costume' and supported by her hand under my chin, I made a valiant effort to stay afloat. Eventually, Mum let go and declared me a swimmer. It was a faltering start and I kept one foot on the bottom of the pool just in case, but at least I did not sink. Diving was a different matter. On the whole I enjoyed being in water, but I just could not drop head first into it while leaving my feet on the edge of the pool.

Mum was not to be deterred and when I was twelve years old and could swim well enough, she summoned me to the deep end of the public pool.

'Come on Miss, I'll teach you to dive.' There were two things wrong with this directive. Firstly, I did not like being called 'Miss'. It spelt 'impatience' in Mum's vocabulary and meant I was in for a harrowing time. Secondly, I did not like her tone which had the hallmarks of a sergeant major on parade. Nonetheless, the moment came when we stood together at the edge of the pool. My white knuckled toes were curled over its rim while Mum coaxed and encouraged me to 'just drop in head first.' After a time she felt her patience fray and then fade altogether. With a sigh she finally cut the lesson short and ordered,

'Just watch me and I'll show you how it's done.' Leaving me on the coping, she sprinted up the steep ladder to the top level of the high dive. I could just make out her form as she balanced on the front edge of the board and bent her knees. Next, she spread her arms wide and, performing a perfect swallow dive, arrowed into the water with hardly a ripple.

'See?' queried a voice at my ear and I turned to find the swimming instructor standing at my side. Pointing a finger in Mum's direction he continued,

'Just copy your big sister and you'll be able to do it as well as she can.'

My father, on the other hand, had an ambivalent relationship with water. Apart from boating and fishing he usually managed to avoid getting wet.

'Why should I take off my warm clothing to immerse myself in cold water when I'm perfectly comfortable as I am?' he would object. Dad never did learn to swim but he had his interests all the same. Apart from fishing, they were generally motorised and needed dry ground with sealed roads for his involvement. Aside from the local doctor, ours was the only car in the village. Everyone else, whether young or old, walked or rode a bicycle. A few had motorbikes with or without sidecars, but in our case, life revolved around the motor vehicle. This was understandable for my father owned a motor business. In those days, not many women took to the wheel but Mum and Dad both drove. This meant driving was an essential part of our family culture and central to our lifestyle. It seemed natural, therefore, that shortly after my fifth birthday Dad should set me up on the edge of an empty fuel can perched on the driver's seat of his Austin 7 with a plan to introduce me to driving. In this way I was elevated enough to see out through the windscreen as I grasped the steering wheel with both hands. Dad sat in the passenger seat beside me and moved the gear stick to neutral. Then, without igniting the engine, we rolled quietly down the hill that led to our front door.

With his foot hovering over the brake and his finger hooked in the base of the steering wheel, he gave a jubilant cry, 'See, you are the driver now!' I thrilled at the notion and laughed with delight as we freewheeled to our destination. In his mind it was a foregone conclusion that one day I would join the driver force and contribute to the family business. In those halcyon days my visual limitation was yet to be known. When it was discovered, stigma joined in to add its dismal scrap to the fabric of my life and to blight the happy carefree hours of childhood.

Sad to say, there was little protection from stigma at school and this was a social hazard. I was sometimes cruelly reminded of my limitation when a classmate put his nose on a printed page and crowed in mock camaraderie, 'Just look, I can read like her!' Sometimes the teasing was merciless with exaggerated and ludicrous gestures. It was especially so if, by someone's reckoning, I moved too close in an effort to recognise who they might be.

'What's the matter, are you blind or something?' was the usual question to precede a torrent of advice.

'You're holding that too close to your eyes,' or 'Why don't you wear glasses?' Nor was I immune from the well-meaning but ill-informed remarks of a teacher,

'Vanity isn't worth the price, wear your glasses, girl!' More than once a well-aimed piece of chalk came hurtling at my head from the hand of a determined master.

It was invariably accompanied by his roar, 'Put on your glasses immediately!' Thankfully, this treatment was occasional rather than frequent and though it stung my body and my pride, it had no lasting impact on my mind. Being of a sanguine temperament, I naturally looked beyond such incidents to the coming of the next bright patch. I knew that when it arrived, it would balance out the undesirable aspects of a day at school.

I must hasten to add that school was not all bad, for I could run like a hare and jump like a doe. It was easy to come second in sporting events that called on these abilities—second, that is, to Ruby Moss. Ruby was an outrageous girl given to shocking social faux pas but she could run. I was tall, but Ruby was taller, and her great long strides made with thin, sinewy of legs won her first prize in every race. Coming second confirmed I had enough speed to combine with considerable spring to gain selection for the inter-schools athletics competition. My performance at the contest was eminently forgettable, however, for I came last in the high jump. Though I did not realise it, I was not sure of the exact height of the bar so I jumped at its approximate position when approximate was not accurate enough. I could have protested that not high, but long jump was really my forte for it had no bar that must be seen from a distance. My sprint was fast and my legs were strong and agile. Surely this would qualify me to succeed in the long jump. With some reluctance Miss McLeod allowed me to try for the event. I stood in line with the other long jump hopefuls. Three went off before me and the sand was raked smooth to remove their imprint after each attempt. Soon it was my turn, and I was on my way with the wind whipping through my hair and my feet gathering speed. All but flying down the field, I leapt at the air above the pit and sailed over the sand below. I landed near the end and Miss McLeod measured my jump with characteristic scepticism.

Then she looked up, incredulity written on her astonished face and exclaimed, 'You've jumped a foot further than your nearest rival!' That day, I revelled in the evident admiration of my peers and even in the fleeting respect I gained from Miss McLeod. If only all life's challenges could end like this. It would make living patchwork such a breeze!

Chapter 3

To Win or Not to Win

If winning was important on the sports field, it was equally as important in other pursuits. In character, our community bore no particular distinction from any other in the province. Like the rest, we were a conservative faith-based village with a keen sense of belonging to one another. In fact, I knew no one, regardless of denomination, who was routinely absent from church on a Sunday. As baby boomer numbers began to swell the population, one small Christian group set up a weekly program for children. In this post-war climate of scarcity, their meeting hall was crowded to capacity with youngsters drawn by the promise of material gain. Every Thursday evening, eager minds absorbed texts and stories from the Bible like blotting paper soaking up excess ink.

A major key to the children's interest lay in the prizes awarded to the winners of quizzes and competitions. 'They're giving out new pencils, even coloured ones with sharpeners, rubbers and rulers to anyone who gets the answers right,' crowed Donna as she rounded up some new recruits to join the gathering throng.

Attending the weekly meeting was 'the thing to do' for any child in the community and I was as enthusiastic as the rest. By mid-primary school, memorisation had become an art form for me—a skill I could call on with ease. During the course of the year, I found I could listen to the stories I had heard and retain them, as well as commit to memory all twenty-six Bible verses assigned. Far from onerous, this amounted to one text per fortnight. The first started with a word that began with the letter 'A'. The second began with a word starting with 'B' and so on through the alphabet to 'Z'. So it was no surprise that most Thursday evenings saw me win at least one prize, if not two, from the coveted stationery cache.

At the end of the year, Superintendent McGuinness stood beaming as he made his annual speech, 'We're planning a party for all of you.' Then, waiting for the roar of approval to subside, he spoke on, 'There'll be plenty of delicious food with cakes and sweets and lemonade.'

Next, young Mr Campbell effused, 'We know you've enjoyed the Bible quizzes and competitions we've held each week and many of you have won prizes. Did you know there's still a grand prize to be won? It'll be awarded at the party to any boy or girl who can recite all twenty-six Bible verses for the year.' Eyes bright with anticipation, many of us determined to come to the party prepared. We would polish up on the texts we had learnt over the months and be ready to recite them. Finally, the day for the party arrived and the food was beyond expectation. Cream cakes and jelly sweets, iced buns and lemonade drinks decked the laden tables where boys and girls surged in to feast. My mother was a fine cook but many community children had never seen such fancy fare. Making the most of it, they buried their faces in the sumptuous treats till all were sated and content.

At length, Mr Campbell rose to his feet and addressed the crowd, 'Now it's time to award a grand prize to anyone who can recite, word perfect, the twenty six Bible verses from memory.'

In reality, if a youngster happened to get stuck and forget the sequence, the alphabet served as a merciful prompt. A hush fell on the room as we waited to see who would be first. Some older boys jumped to their feet to meet the test. A few succeeded in reciting the whole whilst others faltered and sat down deflated. I waited nervously until nearly everyone who wanted to make the attempt had done so and Mr Campbell was calling, 'Is there anyone else who'd like to take a turn?' It was now or never.

Slowly I rose to my feet and began, 'A "Ask, and it shall be given you; seek, and ye shall find; knock and it shall be opened unto you" (Mt 7:7). B "Be not overcome of evil but overcome evil with good" (Rom 12:21). C "Come unto me all ye who labour and are heavy laden and I will give you rest" (Mt 11:28).' Doggedly I persisted with one text after another, glad of the alphabetic prompt to keep me on course. Finally, I finished with 'Z' and sank into my seat with relief. The approval in Mr McGuinness's voice was substantial as he called me forward and awarded me a grand prize. It was a hardcover copy of the biography of Mary Slessor, intrepid missionary to Africa. As I left the hall my nine year old heart soared at the palpable praise of young and old. I loved the positive piece it added to my living patchwork and I luxuriated with delight in the joy of it.

Inevitably, primary school morphed into high school and with it came a consciousness of gender. Given our ethical background, our youthful behaviour was predictably chaste though we were well aware of the opposite sex. An exchange of lingering looks and shy smiles was not uncommon while the occasional 'love' note was passed between us. The highlight of the year was the Christmas party. It was held simultaneously in every church hall in the district and gave opportunity for teenage boys and girls to meet and signal their interest in one another. Games were designed to facilitate contact between the gathered youth where blushing girls held hands for the first time with bashful boys,

'Let's have "The Grand Old Duke of York,"' a voice would call from the platform,

'Come on boys, find a partner and form a line.' Eventually, reticent boys would be encouraged or cajoled into crossing the floor to invite the girls to join them. Once the band had struck up the familiar tune, the column of singing couples would parade through an archway of elevated arms hoping to escape capture. When the music abruptly stopped, the arch would fall locking couples in. If caught like this, the boys would be 'forced' to plant a peck on their partner's cheek before they were free to continue the march. That is, if coyness did not prevent them.

I was almost fifteen the Christmas I attended my first parish party and I best remember those games that brought the keenest embarrassment. Needless to say, these were usually sight dependent. I recall one in particular where we girls sat on a circle of chairs facing inwards with a boy standing behind each chair. One chair was left vacant and the boy standing behind it quickly winked at any girl he chose. The girl responded by attempting to dash from her chair to the one in front of him, while the boy standing behind tried to prevent her from leaving. Imagining I had detected a wink, I dashed without restraint to the chair of a surprised young man who had not moved an eyelid. Inversely, I felt hands of restraint on my shoulders when someone did wink, but I failed to move. I do not think I ever did get it right and the entire circle was highly amused at my inept responses. I did not experience any high level of amusement myself and things were made worse by the question of one of the boys, 'What are you blushing for?' At this, I could feel the colour intensify that was already burning in my cheeks as my embarrassment rose to even greater heights. But, what was the mechanism for this and why could I remember it so well? Many years later a psychology professor would throw some light on the phenomenon.

'We remember an experience best when it is accompanied by heightened emotion. This is because emotion sears the experience into our memory and we retain it,' he said. At this rate, I thought, we can be left remembering negative experiences for life. Because of this, I could expect the dark piece in my living patchwork to predominate and threaten to cast an indelible shadow over my brighter days.

If this dismal fragment cost me comfort, it was small compared with the cost to my Mum and Dad. About this time, they made up their minds to leave Northern Ireland. They had reached this decision because as the local people claimed, 'It rains three hundred days a year and drips off the trees the other sixty five.'

Dad complained and Mum agreed, 'Wouldn't it be nice to live where the sky is blue and the sun shines more often than not?' Their search led them to one of two places on the globe. They would go to Durban in South Africa or Perth in Western Australia.

'Which do you think has more hours of sunshine in an average year?' quizzed Dad. Mum and I admitted ignorance so we tossed a coin and Perth was the winner. The health check to qualify for a £10 passage aboard an English ocean liner was easily passed by my parents. It meant three weeks of near luxury sailing with daily entertainment and exotic port stops along the way. But there was bad news too. It came from the examining doctor who approached Mum and Dad with a serious expression on his face.

'I'm sorry but your daughter hasn't passed the medical

examination. Her vision is too poor for her to be granted an assisted passage. She's fifteen years old so if she goes with you, you'll have to pay a full adult fare for her.' A full adult fare amounted to several hundred pounds and without question my good parents paid it. Though I had little idea of what was in store, excitement born of happy anticipation filled me at the prospect of a new adventure. I was going to the other side of the world and there would be much to discover on the way.

'What will it be like Dad?' I ventured. 'We'll just have to wait and see won't we?' was his standard reply. As it happened, none of us knew very much in making this transition of a lifetime. There were the few British jokes about Australian culture and some anecdotes of friends who had visited the land. As it turned out, we proved to be ill-prepared and uninformed as to the true nature of our move. Each of us in our own sphere was to confront several waves of disappointed expectation until the strange and the new finally became more familiar.

Firstly, school presented a serious challenge for me. No longer the recipient of the British government scholarship, I was enrolled in Form 3 of a public high school that was fee free. When I began to attend, there were still some months to go before Form 3 sat the Junior Certificate examination and I found much of the curriculum quite foreign. After a few weeks I came home with the observation,

'They're away ahead of me in maths and science, but in French and Latin they're a long way behind.' Textbooks for subjects I could normally manage like English and Geography were quite different from what I had known and I had never heard of a component called 'Australian history'. It was all too strange and new and anxiety took hold of me as I had never known it.

'Please, please take me back to Northern Ireland and I'll be a model student,' I begged my parents. '...or at least, let me go back to live with Donna!' I suggested this despite the regime of her rigid mother.

'There's no going back,' pronounced Dad with uncharacteristic firmness. 'We've burned our bridges and like it or not, we're in Australia to stay.' Temporary relief came when the school decided I should drop back a year to prepare for the Third Form exam. The solution was to put me in Second Form with the fourteen year olds.

'I feel like an adult amongst children,' I vociferously complained to Mum, but the worst was yet to come. Second Form provided one teacher only for all subjects. This meant we spent most of the day with Mr Green and I did not relate to him well. One morning he swaggered into class and directed us to note the information written on the blackboard. Moving methodically across the rows, he asked each pupil a question based on the blackboard material. All too soon, it was my turn. I waited as long as I could and then murmured,

'I'm sorry Sir, I can't see the blackboard.' A deathly silence pervaded the room while I underwent interrogation.

'If you can't see through those lenses, isn't it about time you had your glasses changed?' he charged.

'I'm sorry Sir, but glasses don't change what I can see,' I defensively confessed. At this Mr Green perched one buttock on the front of his desk and, ignoring my response, pointed to a boy in the back left corner of the room.

'Well Jamieson, can you see what is written on the blackboard?'

'Yes Sir,' was the eager-to-please reply.

'Good, then read it to the class,' and with flawless fluency Jamieson read. Turning back to me, Mr Green imperiously insisted, 'How is it that a boy sitting in the back row of the classroom has no trouble reading and you're unable to do it while seated in the front row?' Without waiting for an answer he continued, 'I'm afraid this level of education may be beyond you.' Then, with a sad, slow nod of his head he concluded, 'Perhaps you should consider leaving school.'

Memory of the eye specialist's advice on my future employment potential began to flood my mind, 'I suggest an outdoor career for your daughter—perhaps accompanying a van driver to make daily deliveries of milk or bread,' said Dr Braithwaite.

Though leaving school was a welcome suggestion from the Form Two teacher, the thought of running from house to house with bread or milk did not seem a valid career aspiration. With my extra height and slim build, career aspiration did take me to the city modelling school and they tried me out on the catwalk.

Scrutinising my figure with some distain, the assessor remarked, 'You have potential, but you can't afford to add an extra ounce. At the moment, you only just qualify for training as a model.' Despite its apparent glamour, I could see that modelling clothes would fail to offer much by way of a long term career so I began to think again.

'What about a job as a receptionist—you know, the person on the front desk in a firm somewhere. You'd do that well,' suggested Mum. However, receptionists needed training in office skills as well, so I found myself enrolled in a commercial college to learn shorthand, typing and bookkeeping. Shorthand was easily mastered at 120 words per minute but typing was a challenge. How was I going to see what I had to type? It was Dad who came to the rescue by making an ingenious device. Its base was a heavy car wheel hub and cap. To this, the flexible arm of a reading lamp had been fitted and a flat metal plate screwed to its top where the lamp would normally have been. This meant I could clip my work to the plate and extend the flexible arm towards my eyes until it was near enough to read. Able to see my work, I achieved a speed of 100 words per minute—enough to apply for a job. Not that I had overcome the presence of the rough dark patch but, far from dispelling it from my life, I was learning to live with, and around it as best I could.

Despite every effort, however, living around it was not always possible. I was sixteen when the tyranny of this fragment loomed even larger. It grew to insurmountable proportions when the day arrived for Dad to teach me to drive.

'Come girls,' he addressed Mum and me, 'Let's go up north on a quiet country road and have a driving lesson.' I had known the theory of driving ever since I could remember, so it was just a matter of practising what I knew under Dad's direction. Mum climbed into the back of the car and Dad sat beside me in the front passenger seat. I started the engine, engaged the gears and was gathering speed on a grey dust road through a stretch of grey/green bush. As we neared the top of a modest hill my father cautioned,

'Just pull out around him now.' I instinctively obeyed passing a small grey utility parked on the side of the road. At a safe distance beyond the vehicle I slowed to a halt and pulling up, switched off the engine.

'I didn't see him,' I blurted. 'Had you not spoken, Dad, I'd have driven straight into the back of him.' I trembled with shock as I climbed out of the driver's seat on two shaky legs. It was a defining moment, for we all knew right then that I could never drive with safety. The realisation was a declaration of doom to an aspiring driver such as I, and the cruelty of the rough dark patch threatened to overwhelm me once again. In times to come my father would live to mourn my visual condition for it would become clear that I had inherited the genetic mutation from him. Though his own expression of the gene was mild enough to be almost imperceptible, mine was much more severe. The gloomy patch also brought a social separation between my friends and me as, one by one, they obtained a licence while I made my way to the bus stop. Certainly, they offered me rides but my fierce sense of autonomy and independence was shattered and the damage could not be repaired. For a time, I lost sight of the rest of the pleasant, appealing fabric present in my living patchwork, and could see only the unwelcome length of coarse dark weave that seemed to dominate the whole.

From my eighteenth birthday on, I considered visits to an eye specialist redundant and depressing. As far as it could go, diagnosis was as complete as medical science could provide and treatment was unavailable. While self-pity offered little attraction, a pleasing resilient updraught came to my aid. It lifted me above the prevailing circumstances and carried me over them. I saw that despite my disability, I did not need to work at establishing a sense of personal worth for its possession was as natural to me as my gender. I knew I was of value and that feeling never left me. Of course, I could not be of value without being of value to someone. To be of value to myself was not enough for, being relational qualities, value and worth are only found reflected in the eyes of another and not in one's own eyes. In other words, personal value is only a reality when it finds its source in someone else's estimation. I was fortunate here, for I found a ready source in my parents' belief in me. Theirs was a 'no strings attached' kind of belief which meant it did not depend on my accomplishments. Rather, it rested on the fact that I was their child and that was enough. With no doubts or conditions to my acceptance with them, I was free to become whatever I chose with only the self-imposed expectations that entailed. Rising to meet these expectations generated self-respect—a much healthier acquisition than self-pity. At the same time I recognised that while parental reinforcement of a positive self-image was a great asset, it was not sufficient to last a lifetime. There had to be something more.

Chapter 4

To Find or not to Find

Indeed there was something more. It arrived as a chain of events that led to a radical life change. The sequence began one evening shortly before we left Ireland. Father had come across a Bible neatly stacked in a bookcase and had sat down to read. After some time, Mother summoned us for the evening meal and Dad emerged from the sitting room wearing a puzzled frown.

Holding the Bible open at the book of Revelation he started to explain: 'I know this book is at the end of the Bible but I thought it might be interesting because of its title. I wondered if it might reveal something I didn't already know. I must admit, I've never read the likes of it before. What do all these strange animals mean and the descriptions of unearthly beings, weird places and odd events? Frankly, it reads like somebody's nightmare and makes me wonder what it's doing in the Bible.' Intrigued at Dad's impression, we sat together by the glowing embers of our winter hearth and read it through together. Ultimately, we closed the Bible admitting we were none the wiser for the exercise.

Soon after our encounter with the odd book at the end of the Bible, we made our move to Australia. It took some months to find a suitable home and when we had bought it, we settled in and ordered a daily delivery of the newspaper. While scanning its contents one evening, Dad exclaimed, 'Well I never!' Avid theatregoers that we were, he had been searching the advertisements in the entertainment section to see if there was anything of interest. With one eyebrow raised in enquiry, he turned to Mum and me, 'Remember our perplexity over that last book in the Bible--Revelation?' We both nodded. 'Well, here's somebody offering to explain it. They're holding a series of lectures in the city—Anzac House, it says. Want to go along?'

'May as well. No one we know seems to understand anything in that weird book,' Mum agreed. The following Wednesday evening found the three of us seated in the public hall and ready to listen. Strange and mysterious though the content of Revelation was, the explanations we heard that night were both startling and plausible while surprisingly down to earth. We continued to attend the lectures finding them to be more interesting than any film on offer. In time, the Bible became relevant, not just as ancient history but as a guide to contemporary living. Though we were not ignorant of its better known stories, our interest in it as a whole, began to grow. Consequently it drew us in, and its teachings moved gradually from the periphery to the centre of our lives. As mystery gave way to meaning and apprehension to joy, we welcomed the transition.

There was something very comforting about the assurance that God actually loved us. Suddenly the past, the present and the future started to hang together in a harmonious whole that appealed to both mind and emotion. To me it was an epiphany, a moment of enlightenment. All at once I knew where I had come from, why I was here and where I was ultimately going. A flashback recalled my confession as a seven-year-old to a strange man on a lonely country road, 'I'm not alone. I'm with Jesus and he's with me.' Age appropriate simplicity had inspired the comment then but there was depth to the conviction, now that I was older, and it drew me on to follow and to serve. Mum kept pace with me and enjoyed a comparable life change to my own. All her days she had sought for something more—reading copiously in her search for understanding and inner peace. At last she had found it.

Dad, however, quickly grasped the implications of our deeper interest in the Bible and drew back. He resisted the life change it implied and opposed us in our continued search. Difficult days followed while a developing rift threatened to force us apart. The happy atmosphere that once pervaded our home gave way to tension and a mild hostility. Even as Dad persevered in dropping descriptors like 'gullible' and 'naive' when he saw demonstration of our sincerity, I began to lose sight of the warm, affectionate man I had always known. I honestly feared the developing family split might intensify and last forever.

'As a family, where do you think these winds of change will leave us?' I tentatively questioned Mum.

'I don't know, Love,' she consoled, 'but I hope we can come through intact, the way we used to be, only better.' Adjustment does not happen overnight and it took two years for the wall of separation to fall down, but I was first to see it. Distributing fresh laundry to various rooms in the house one day, I came upon my father in the bedroom he shared with my mother. He was quietly kneeling beside his bed with his back to the door and was clearly praying. I had never seen him do this before, so I retreated on tiptoe recognising in an instant that something profound was happening. Dad was a private man, so I knew better than to question him on what I had observed. Patience demanded I wait to see what might eventuate and I was not disappointed. Dad grew at his own pace over time and eventually he joined Mum and me in our new way of life. To my delight, the 'new normal' in our home brought beautiful colour and variety to my pieces of living patchwork. Fresh new scraps of soft light texture, tinted with delicate shades, had come to stay adding interest and vitality to the whole. Like so many shafts of sunlight they illuminated life, transforming it into a thing of undeniable appeal. I began to see greater purpose and possibility in living patchwork, despite its unpredictable design.

I longed, of course, that this transformation might also bring physical change in the shape of normal sight. Just one small miracle should not be too much to ask. But there was no miracle, big or small, and despite my prayers, fasting and pledges of obedience, I could see no better.

Finally, I began to bargain with God, 'Surely its plain I could serve you much better if only I had full sight. Countless are the occasions in the Gospels when you healed the sick and disabled including the blind. Many of them were believers and so am I. You asked blind Bartimaeus what he wanted from you. In answer he pled, 'Lord, that I might receive my sight," and you healed him. Well, I'm just another blind Bartimaeus seeking the same response.' There was an answer, but it was different from the one I sought. It was the answer the Apostle Paul received when he prayed three times in desperation wanting his affliction removed, 'My grace is sufficient for you, for my power is made perfect in weakness' (2 Cor. 12:9). I must admit I found it hard to respond to my disability with the spiritual maturity of the great apostle.

He could sincerely say, 'So I will boast all the more gladly of my weaknesses, so that the power of Christ may dwell in me' (2 Cor. 12:9). I was not glad, and it became clear I was to learn to 'walk by faith, not by sight' (2 Cor. 5:7) to a greater degree than I had hoped. Walking by faith was fine. It was what every believer did. But taken literally, 'not by sight' meant times of embarrassment and chagrin when it came to my efforts to see while others watched me struggle. When I used awkward and obvious high-powered magnification in full view of the curious, the inquisitive, and the tactless, I felt myself shrink from their patent gaze. Some, like my cousin Norma, made a brave attempt to comfort me, 'Oh, no one would ever know you had anything wrong with your eyes. You look so…well…normal.' At times like these, a wishful sigh would escape my lips, signalling a desire to be as normal as I looked. Perhaps it was through pride, or some inner strength, but an easy resistance to the temptation to perceive myself as being less of a person than others, came to my rescue. It preserved me from sinking emotionally and helped keep me buoyant. Though unguarded expressions of shock and murmurs of dismay on the part of observers continued to surround me, I acknowledged no defeat. Beyond tokens of sympathy or words of approbation for how capably I could cope, I preferred to be seen as no different from anyone else in the task of managing life. It was important to me that people should forget my limitations while appreciating my accomplishments, and to this end, I bent my energies.

It was not long before opportunity to fulfil this ambition arose. It came when several of my friends announced their intention to move to the other side of the country.

'Our plan is to attend a denominational training college in New South Wales. Norm here wants to be a teacher, Margaret an accountant and Sheryl an office secretary. Tom has the high aspiration to become a minister and Marilyn is keen on being a nurse. Actually, we all want to be missionaries of one kind or another—at home or abroad—doesn't really matter where.' Their fervour was infectious and when I heard their plan, my sense of adventure burst into life once more while enthusiasm gripped me and fired my imagination. I was already a secretary, so what if I went with them and trained to become a ministerial assistant? It was not a novel idea for I had observed a woman in Perth working in this capacity and was strongly attracted to what she did. Amongst other things, it would involve teaching all ages and my students would be people who wanted to understand the Bible better.

'That's right up my alley,' I declared, deciding to join my friends on their journey to greater things. The notion that a woman could aspire to pastoral ministry had entered no one's mind in those days, much less my own. It was clear that ministry was for men, but women could at least assist in some pastoral areas, especially those offering service, if not exerting authority.

The five day journey by train from Perth to Sydney took us across the country to our destination. Two days later, I had registered for the course to qualify me for the coveted role. The level of study was undemanding and I found the course far from exacting. By overloading with some subjects and challenging others through sitting exams without attending classes, I was ready to graduate after two years instead of three. These were years of fun and frolic. Socially, they were highly rewarding, spiritually inspiring, and not very academically challenging. Thus, I had the time of my life developing new friendships and establishing relationships that would last a lifetime.

Amongst my fellow students was a cluster of young sophisticates, women from the city of Sydney, who tutored me informally in the art of dress and haircare.

'Let's blonde our hair,' suggested Barb one lazy Sunday

afternoon. It was a bold suggestion for 'good girls' did not colour their hair on our particular campus. Debra overcame our hesitation by adding, 'I dare you.' That was enough to send us scurrying for the blonding cream. When we had done the deed and towelled off, Val inspected our heads and anxiously exclaimed, 'Oh no, it's far too brassy!'

'Better use this,' advised phlegmatic Bev, holding aloft a small jar the size of an eye-drop bottle and containing a purple fluid.

'Look, here are the instructions,' announced Jan, 'it says to use five drops in a jug of rinsing water.

'That should tone down the brass nicely,' concluded Pam and I joined the bevy of brassy blondes in a communal sigh of relief. Patiently I awaited my turn with the small bottle of purple tint and its dainty dropper. With five heads successfully subdued to a natural looking ash blonde, I took the bottle and squeezed the drops into the jug of water. I was careful to add extra drops because my fine, naturally mid-blonde hair had taken tenaciously to the blonding cream and was exceptionally brassy. After some minutes, there was an obvious result with indelible effect. I was crowned with a halo of bright purple hair and no amount of scrubbing would modify the colour. Though purple was not usually an easy colour for me to see, the bright magenta mass was inescapable, even to my eyes. It was clearly not the way to gain appreciation for my accomplishments but it did attract a good deal of attention and it took months to live the folly down. Years after, at a dinner party or in a concert hall, a familiar comment would sometimes float across the space between a scarcely remembered acquaintance and me, 'Weren't you the girl with the purple hair in our second year?'

If the acquisition of purple hair was not to be repeated, I wish I could say the same for living dangerously with water. It was true water had played a challenging role in my girlhood, but when I had just turned twenty, it became a greater threat. Our first year at the college was introduced by a particularly rainy autumn. My friend Lyn and I shared a first-floor dormitory room where our window offered an unobstructed rural view. Below us flowed a gentle river skirted by a stretch of bushland with walking tracks allotted to female students. In a normal season the river flowed lazily beneath a low footbridge, but this year, it lapped over the bridge and was slowly climbing up its banks.

On a whim, I suggested to Lyn, 'Let's go and visit Pete and Trish this afternoon before the track floods and prevents us from getting through.' Pete was a married student living with his wife in a cottage at the end of the bushland. They had travelled from Perth a month or two before us, and when homesickness threatened to bite a little harder than usual; they were a tangible link with the past that promised a touch of the familiar.

'Good idea,' Lyn agreed while we donned clear plastic raincoats and pulled on Wellington boots. Splashing through the mud, we made it to the end of the bushland and reached the cottage in good time.

'Oh, do come in,' called Trish as Pete held the door open for us. 'Come and have a hot drink and some biscuits. It's always good to see you girls.' We reminisced together over a cup of cocoa in the comfort of their cosy living room. We talked about the past and the people we knew, as well as the present with its new acquaintances. All the while, the rain gushed down in sheets outside. Feeling better for the cheering visit we stood to take our leave knowing that thirty minutes at most would see us back in the dorm.

Skipping along in happy conversation about our friends, we did not notice the difference in the bushland track until we were halfway along it. By then it was obvious the river had overflowed its banks and was covering the track. As we progressed the water deepened. Soon it was too late to turn back and there was no way forward unless we waded. We were now closer to the dormitory than to Trish and Pete's cottage so we kept on wading while the rain continued to fall. In a matter of minutes the gentle river had become a torrent reaching up to our waists and then to our chests as it caught us in its flow and washed us into the midstream current.

'We'll have to swim for it,' I yelled above the roar of the water. As we launched into the deep, weeds, saplings and vines clawed at our legs, determined to hold us back and drag us under. Washed helplessly downstream, we grabbed at any tree that might halt our forceful drift as we panted for breath in the struggle to stay afloat. Nearing panic, we called to each other that the bank we were desperately trying to reach could not be far away. In truth, however, strength was giving out and fatigue was hindering our progress. Suddenly, a human form appeared on an elevation just ahead and a voice called, 'Over here, keep coming, you're nearly there.' A pair of strong hands firmly grasped first Lyn and then me, and hauling us up, dragged us above the waterline and onto the bank. For some minutes we lay exhausted and motionless on the wet grass, still wrapped in our plastic raincoats and resembling a recent purchase from the local fish market. Squinting up at our rescuer we recognised him to be Lyn's boyfriend. The fast-flowing river had washed us downstream near the grassy field that lay at the foot of his parents' home. Without knowing who we were, he had spied two people in difficulty in the swollen flood and had come to help.

I could call this a funny little scrap in my living patchwork for we could laugh about it—after the event at any rate. At the time, it was alarming to say the least. It could not honestly be aligned with my big dark patch for it had nothing to do with eyesight and the folly was my own creation. It did, however, have everything to do with heightened fear and the sense of relief that comes from being rescued. As it was, thanks to a boyfriend, we did survive to tell the tale.

Chapter 5

To Love or not to Love

Finding a boyfriend was a known expectation—an informal part of the college curriculum for most of us. Lyn managed it in our first week of study and then moved on to a second and a third romantic attachment. Finally, she married none of them. My success with boyfriends was much less spectacular. Having decided that mutual attraction is a delicate thing, I did not succeed at finding a boyfriend until the very last week of college. I confess I had not lacked for admirers, but I was either too slow on the uptake to benefit from their interest, or simply too hard to please.

There were, on the other hand, the honeypot girls. Around these, young men swarmed like bees with marriage in their sights. Honeypot girls were routinely snapped up by successful suitors and led to the altar a week or two after graduation. Next to them were the plainer girls whose appeal lay in their bright personalities and witty repartee. Social desirability made these girls attractive to men as entertaining friends, but there was little romantic interest. To complete the complement there were odd girls, socially awkward girls, shy retiring girls, those who were altogether too eager and those who were much too aloof. The dormitory was home to all.

As it turned out, the gender equation was in balance for similar descriptions as these applied to the boys as well. They were just as diverse as the girls and it posed a problem for everyone. The culture of the day decreed that a man must take the initiative in approaching a woman as a first step towards a romantic relationship. On the other hand, a woman could not approach a man for this purpose and, at the same time, retain her respectability. Culture had pinned us all securely down in our gender roles and it seemed to us girls that the boys had the better of it. The boys, however, did not always agree with this for society frowned on the casual date and only approved the serious advance. A boy might have been attracted to a particular girl, but shoring up the courage to ask her out on a first date was quite another thing. Many a fellow shook in his boots at the very thought of failure. For some, reticence ruled from fear of outright rejection or for being made feel foolish. Reticence was hazardous, however, when it led to dangerous delays. By procrastinating, the reticent boy could face keen disappointment if, having plucked up enough courage to approach the girl of his choice, he was outstripped by a rival in pursuit of the same girl. In this sense, the vagaries of the dating game provided disincentives for many a young man.

Staying by these gender protocols spelt limitation for me. I may have hoped for the romantic interest of a young man who appealed to me but I could not pursue him. Instead I waited, like a good girl should, until I was rewarded one day with an unexpected surprise. I had picked up my washing from the campus laundry, and on my return to the dormitory, found John standing in the foyer. John was an immigrant from Germany, a painter by trade and a second-year ministerial student. Up to that moment, our contact had usually been within a group. There were classes we had taken together, outreach programs we had supported and the ministerial club where we were active members. We had also had a few chance meetings when John was repainting the girls' dormitory and I had stopped to chat. John was popular with the girls. They liked his European charm, the easy way he related to women in general, and his sympathetic attention as they poured their troubles into his listening ear. Besides, having a kind of 'understanding' with an Italian girl in Sydney, he was not seeking a relationship with anyone at the college. This gave him freedom to be friends with us all without being misunderstood. On this occasion, John and I exchanged a casual 'hello' in the hallway and I made to move on but he continued to speak,

'We were wondering if you'd like to come out to dinner with us this evening.' Clearly, this was a collective invitation and I stood wondering which group from amongst our mutual connections could be getting together. I guessed that, seeing graduation was just one week away, the dinner was probably a farewell gesture.

'Sure,' I casually replied, 'Who are they?'

'Well, actually, um…it's just me.' This was beginning to sound suspiciously like a date and I rushed in with,

'Oh, do you mean just you and me?' Along with his admission, a pink flush coloured his cheeks.

'That's what I had in mind.'

'Ah,' I exclaimed and my thoughts crowded in as I silently wondered if mutual attraction had come at last. I certainly liked John and was attracted to him but what about Simona in Sydney? What was the status of his relationship with her? So, I broke the silence with the half-formed question,

'…and Simona?'

'I no longer have a particular friendship with Simona,' he reassured. 'I went down to Sydney last weekend and ended what there was between us.' More silence followed for a moment while I digested this. Then, as though encouraged by a recollection, he continued,

'So you see, I'm quite free to ask you out.' Though his words generated some sympathy for Simona, relief flooded my mind at his candour. I suspected he was a young man of moral substance whose straightforward intentions could be trusted, and I accepted his invitation.

What a splendid addition this made to my living patchwork and there were some welcome pieces yet to come. Everything I could wish was falling into place. The last week of the academic year had become the week of realised dreams. Exams over, John and I were inseparable for the seven days until my graduation. During this time I was offered an assistant ministerial position in New Zealand. To add to my joy, the verses I had submitted in the competition to select the graduating class poem were declared the winner. I was euphoric!

Because of its emotional nature, euphoria has a finite lifetime and what goes up must inevitably come down. It was moving to New Zealand that effected an immediate change in my mood. Relocation meant separation by sea from everyone I knew and loved. It awakened the dormant threat of loneliness familiar to an only child. I knew the way to overcome this was to make new friends. The question was, would the New Zealanders welcome me, or would it prove hard to break through their natural reserve? Only time would tell.

I arrived at Auckland airport late on a summer evening fully expecting to be met as arranged. It was my first landing in this strange new country with its native fauna and flora. In this place, nature was complemented by a musical Maori culture that differed from anything I had ever known. Though otherwise accented, the familiar sound of my mother tongue hovered on the lips of these total strangers. This helped enormously for at least I could easily communicate. As time moved the day of my arrival beyond its sunset and left me in the darkness of night, it was obvious no one had come to meet me. Despite the disappointment that accompanies a letdown, apprehension was slow in coming for I was secure in the knowledge that I was now twenty-one years old and well able to take care of myself. So I stood outside the small Whenuapai terminal, suitcase in hand, as midnight struck and the last remaining taxi was pulling away from the curb. The driver hesitated for a moment and then stopped to warn,

'When I leave, you'll be here on your own... better come with me. I can take you somewhere to stay for the night.' He dropped me off at a comfortable B&B and next morning, I phoned my new employer. He was a brusque north Englishman, who, on learning my name, roundly chastised me for not communicating my arrival time,

'How come you didn't inform us of your flight time? You should have forwarded your arrival details and we would have made sure you were met at the airport,' was the essence of his reprimand. Uncomfortable though it was, this exchange gave me an insight for it made me realise that effective communication is a rare skill, claimed by many but exercised by few.

'I did send a message through the church entity that booked my ticket,' I protested, but he did not seem to hear. Feeling diminished, I replaced the receiver and wondered if my excitement over this new position might have been somewhat misplaced. The disadvantage of having been treated with the unmitigated acceptance and positive regard of my earlier years was to leave me vulnerable and ill-prepared for this kind of reception. Unhappy and deflated, I was collected from my night's lodgings and deposited in the care of a local pastor under whose direction I was charged to work for the next two years.

Pastor M. was an affable, cultured gentleman with a British colonial heritage. He exhibited the old world grace and good manners of his kind and reminded me strongly of my English father. We were located in the medium-sized regional city of Hamilton on the Waikato River with a population of 55,000. These days the city boasts three times that and I would be expected to buy a car to carry me from one address to another to make home calls. In 1964, however, a pushbike was considered adequate, so I bought a sturdy model from a second-hand shop and set off to visit the people on my list. In order to find my way around, I needed to memorise a map of the district and match it to the actual streets. The task of reading street signs was a challenge for me. They were simply too far away to see so my bicycle doubled as a stepladder. Resting it against the signpost, I mounted it, climbing up from the outer pedal to stand with both feet on the saddle. Stretching up, I was able to read the name that appeared just above my head. In this way, I managed to locate the addresses for those I planned to visit.

Though it might have suited the foolhardy, visiting was not for the faint-hearted. On the whole, women were easy to visit, warmly welcoming my company and the spiritual encouragement I brought to them. More than once, however, I was alarmed by a well-meaning man who invited me in, securely locked and bolted the door behind me and positioned himself between me and any means of escape. In some cases the action was prompted by pure absent-mindedness and was followed by profuse and embarrassed apology. But in others, I am not so sure. Thankfully, I managed to ease my way out of more scary situations unscathed and without having to make the demand,

'Let me out of here!' As a result, both they and I retained our dignity.

By the time I had landed in New Zealand, I had a new improved version of the typing stand my father had constructed years before. I now put it to use typing lecture notes and letters for my boss. Developing my own sermons was easy enough. I simply put the material together and memorised it, to deliver it later without notes. Thus my visual limitation was not an obstacle, not to me, nor to my boss, nor to the girls and young women under my spiritual care. As my leadership skills developed, the girls began to see me as a role model and then as a mentor. In this way, several useful fragments in the form of emerging maturity came to join my living patchwork.

Gathering new friends In New Zealand proved easier than I had thought and working from a church base served to help the process along. In all, my close social group amounted to six. There was Irene and Marjorie, nurses at the local hospital and Vicky, an accountant, who became my flatmate. Two school teachers, Alana and Petra, known to me already in Australia came to New Zealand and it was not difficult to renew old ties with them. In addition, there was Bruce who was quite comfortable in our social sisterhood. I soon learned he had six sisters and no brothers and was convinced this accounted for his ease in belonging to us! As a bonus, Pastor and Mrs M. had four grown children and, in terms of age, I fitted neatly between the second and third. It so happened that just before my arrival, their parental nest had undergone a severe emptying and no one was left but a teenage girl about to enter boarding school. My arrival helped to soften the severity of the grief they suffered from the absence of their older children. Thus they eagerly absorbed me into their family and treated me like a daughter. I found this more than acceptable because it meant I was not overwhelmed by an instant clan of newly acquired siblings. Instead, I had company enough in a peaceful place, where a certain positive regard, healthy attention and warm support enveloped me. This was what Pastor and Mrs M. had given their offspring and, in my view, it made for a satisfactory arrangement.

Mrs M. loved children and over time she helped me shed my mother's notion that they were a nuisance to be avoided if possible or, at best, endured.

'If you don't have children, you only know the half of life,' she had caution. 'To have children is to live life twice—once for yourself and once again through them.' Gleaned from experience more than books, she freely shared her homespun wisdom. A fine cook, good gardener and superb seamstress, Mrs M. was the epitome of housewifely skill and blessed with more than a modicum of propriety. My engagement to John prompted her to bring out a book she had discreetly stowed somewhere out of sight. Shyly she presented it to me. The volume was modestly clothed in a brown paper jacket to hide its actual identity.

'As each of my children becomes engaged to be married, I lend them this book to help them understand the nature of married life,' she confided. 'You may borrow it if you like.' I was intrigued and took the book guessing from her demeanour that it must be about sex. The sexual revolution of the later 1960s had not yet dawned, so sex was a delicate topic and I admired Mrs. M. for even broaching it with me. I was keen enough to read the book, but alas, found it to be so full of subtle elusions and flowery euphemisms that I was no more informed about sex when I finished reading it than I had been when I began.

For my second year in New Zealand, Pr and Mrs M. and I moved from Hamilton to Palmerston North in Manawatu. Here I took a room in the home of an elderly widow, Mrs B. I continued to work for Pastor M. caring for his correspondence, visiting people who had signed up to learn more about the Bible and making the occasional public presentation. Although Mrs B. and I were the sole occupants of her brick and weatherboard house, our obvious vulnerability generated no fear of danger, that is, until one wintry night in August.

I had gone to bed and was sleeping as soundly as any young person who had spent three hours of the working day peddling a bicycle. It was around midnight when I realised with a jolt that I was standing upright in the middle of the bedroom floor and the overhead light was on. I did not recall being woken up nor remember getting out of bed. So, baffled and confused, I remained there as I slowly came to full consciousness. Certain by this time that I must have been dreaming, I switched off the light and climbed back into bed. Then I heard it, a loud knocking on the front door. Fully alert, I stiffened and climbing out of bed, crawled out through my bedroom door and across the hallway floor on my hands and knees in the darkness. While doing this, I passed the front door where an upper pane of frosted glass revealed the sharp outline of a man silhouetted in the moonlight. He was wearing a heavy overcoat and a homburg hat. Making noiselessly for Mrs. B.'s bedroom I found her lying anxiously awake. Laying a trembling hand on my arm she queried,

'What is it?' and I whispered unwisely,

'It's a man.'

'Oh dear, what are we going to do?' she quavered, fear mounting quickly in her voice.

'I'll crawl back into the hallway and call the police,' I offered.

'Yes, yes, good idea,' she nervously agreed. Assured by the

constable that help was on its way, I replaced the receiver and started back towards my bedroom. Just then a familiar voice boomed an Urdu greeting from the porch on the other side of the front door,

'Missahib, are you there?' it called.

'Pastor M!' I gasped in dismay and tightening the sash of my dressing gown made to open the door. At the same time, two policemen jogged into position—one on each side of the beleaguered pastor while they ignored his voluble protests. Helplessly I stood on the doorstep trying to understand the scene before me. After a pause, one of the policemen asked,

'Do you know this man?'

'Y-Yes, I stammered. He's my boss.'

'Do you need our assistance?'

'No!' cried Pastor M. but the officer fixed his gaze on me and waited for my response. With all the composure I could muster I declared,

'It's quite all right, officer. We didn't realise who was at the door and thought it best to call you. We will be fine now.' Once the police had withdrawn, Pastor M. set about explaining his midnight call,

'There's been a bad accident. A family travelling down from Auckland was involved in a car crash. Unfortunately, the mother died at the scene and one of the children has severe head injuries—father is also in hospital. Two children are OK and are being discharged soon. When I bring them home, I need you to be in the house to care for them while I return to the hospital.' Tossing on some day clothes, I jumped into the car and we took off for the family's deserted dwelling. Once inside, I lost no time in lighting the gas fire and checking to see what could be used for breakfast when the time came. Soon the two small children arrived, bewildered and half asleep. They were not really aware of what had befallen them so, with a little persuasion, they settled down quietly in familiar beds. In no time they were fully asleep, slumbering away the early morning hours towards a new day with its harsh unwelcome reality. Though I could ultimately walk away from this and put my hand to other needs, that night delivered a grim swatch to be added to my living patchwork. Awful as it was, it taught me first-hand the meaning of empathy with the suffering of my world and ultimately turned my feet toward a ministry that would support them.

CHAPTER 6

To Know or not to Know

When I was not harassed by homesickness or beset with longing for the company of John, I recognised a certain truth. It dawned on me that pleasant experiences in congenial surroundings conspire over time to make a person feel at home. This sums up the effect New Zealand had on me. I developed a sense of loyalty to this land and if I were to choose a national rugby team to support, it would be the All Blacks, even today! As for the land, I delighted in its pastoral scenes where flocks of Romney sheep flecked the rolling hills that were mantled in lush green grass while near the groups of close-cropped ewes, clusters of woolly lambs gambolled in the spring. On the shores of glassy lakes, giant tussock grasses of toetoe waved their creamy flower plumes while snow-capped mountains cast their image on still, clear water below. Amongst the trees of the native bush the complex song of the tui rang whilst the flightless weka hiked the trails and the kea called from lofty alpine heights. Beneath the earth, glow worms shone like tiny lamps in the depths of darkened limestone caves. Closely packed, they studded walls and ceilings like myriads of stars in an underground Milky Way. In geothermal hotspots boiling water shot thirty metres high from steaming geysers several times a day, while seething sulphurous mud pools lured the careless, man and beast, to a torrid end. The splendour of peak and sound, where glacial rivers of solid ice fell in slow descent to melt and flow with quickened pace in stony valleys below, held my gaze in fascinated wonder. Though I did not realise it then, it was an ideal time to appreciate the unspoiled beauty of this land. It is no surprise that in decades yet to come, tourists would flock to rename it: 'The Switzerland of the southern hemisphere'. As for living patchwork, my days in New Zealand added a certain splendour to the collage I was crafting and it became a reference point to draw me back to its beauty for frequent visits in future years.

If leaving these islands caused grief, returning to Australia generated joy. For one thing, I was a much better cyclist, physically fitter by far and some kilos lighter than when I had left. For another, I was reuniting with everyone I loved, especially John. Landing in Sydney, I caught a train to my alma mater and arrived in time for his graduation. It was not actually two years since we had been together. Halfway through my days in New Zealand, he had come to work there for the summer months and before he returned to Australia we had announced our engagement. By the time another year had passed, wedding bells were in the air and we could hardly wait for the day to arrive. We had to wait, however, for John was enrolled in a post-graduate course for eight weeks while I flew home to Perth to prepare for our great celebration. In this way, pieces of lace, yards of organza and clouds of wispy tulle blended together in delicate design to advance the creation of all I desired in my living patchwork.

It was that time of life when youth overcomes all obstacles and love is ever blind. In keeping with this, my visual defect diminished in significance. I did not permit it to pose a problem for me, nor did it seem to bother John. Self-reliance and independence were the more prominent features of my personality and I despised self-pity. Still, I did need John's reassurance and one evening I looked for it. Shortly before our wedding, we took a stroll on a sandy beach as the heat of the day abated. On the western horizon the setting sun was a ball of liquid fire as it slowly dipped into a luminous sea. The air was warm and the breeze gentle when I turned to John.

'Does it trouble you that I can't see very well?' I ventured.

He smiled and drawing me close, whispered, 'It wasn't your eyesight that attracted me.' Laughing, we clasped hands and sprinted along the water's edge where tiny wavelets broke on the golden shore, secure in the knowledge that 'love conquers all'. Whether it actually did or not remained to be seen. Living patchwork may yet teach me the need to draw on reserves of resilience as we went on our wedded way. This would no doubt mean enjoying the highs and negotiating the lows of a terrain familiar to many a married pair.

By the time we did marry, it had been six years since John had left Germany for Australia and his parents, Papa and Mutti to us, were keen to see their son again.

'They'd like us to stay for a year, but I can't imagine that, unless I work while we're there,' John announced. As a wedding gift, Papa offered to pay our passage to Europe on an Italian liner. Stopping at several ports *en route*, it would take six weeks to reach Genoa from Fremantle. We were already inclined to accept the offer when he sent us another letter.

'We've set up a new apartment for you on our ground floor. If you're willing to come, it's yours rent-free for as long as you like.' To my mind, this was the stuff of fairy tales but, like breakfast in bed, it was a lovely idea with the potential to become awkward and uncomfortable. To overcome the peril inherent in fully depending on his parents, John took up an offer to work in pastoral ministry where he earned a modest stipend for most of the year. This suited his personality and it also pleased his father for they held the belief in common that 'to live is to work'. Nor was I to escape this family ethic for, soon after our arrival, Papa used the endearment shared by John and me to broach the subject of my employment.

'I have a good job for you too, Sweetie. You can come and work for me as an English language stenographer. My correspondence is mostly with America and you'll be a great help. I'll pay you well.' He smiled in expectation of my grateful acceptance. I had my own agenda, however, for the time I would be living in Germany and it did not include working in the English language.

'That's very kind of you Papa,' I responded, 'but I want to spend my time here learning the culture, the cuisine and how to cook it, and the language. I want to be amongst Germans absorbing all I can from them.' Surprised, if not shocked by my refusal to work which I doubt he understood, he respected my wish and urged no more.

'Oh well,' he concluded, 'If you change your mind, the job's still on offer.' Free to follow my own plans and from the practical experience I had gained in New Zealand, I accompanied John as coach, teaching him the art of pastoral visitation. When possible, I spent my days in language classes or in private tuition honing the skills I hoped to master. We also led a busy social life with plenty of opportunity to entertain--German youth from the church, American soldiers stationed nearby, friends from John's past, friends from Australia and New Zealand travelling through or living in Europe and John's employers.

A step that gave impetus to my learning German was my enrolment at night school in a course called, 'German for

Foreigners'. It was the first time in my life I had been classified as 'foreign' but it helped me realise how non-English speakers migrating to Australia must feel as they attempt to integrate with the locals. I knew, too, that as an adult one must learn a foreign language formally. Just 'picking it up' was for young children but this art eluded the adult who would speak a poor version of the language unless formally taught. This said, the course at night school proved more entertaining than educative. During our many weeks at sea, John had given me a crash course in German that resulted in a rudimentary knowledge. This helped as I was the only native English speaker enrolled in the class which consisted mainly of Spanish and Italian migrant workers. The teacher, an endlessly patient old retiree, laboured tirelessly to improve our grasp of the language by instructing us in a clear precise German. We, on the other hand, could only communicate with one another in German. For some time, our attempts amounted to a fragmentary smattering of the tongue interspersed with long pauses and some giggles. Mostly we resorted to sign language with a few guttural gurgles that we hoped passed for German. I learned a lot about Spaniards and Italians so the exercise was culturally enriching if not so linguistically productive. It was really John who taught me most of what I mastered during that year. Patiently, he corrected my faulty grammar and pronunciation and explained similarities and differences from English that made learning German easier. I took a little pride in smoothing out his English here and there but there really was no comparison between our levels of competence. All the while I was adding new dimensions to living patchwork and it was good fun. Language learning was an auditory rather than a visual skill so I enjoyed it as a pleasant patch to be integrated into the whole.

For a person who had never lived in an English speaking country, Papa's English was superior. Generous spirited in big things, his thrift and frugality were only apparent in small things and provided me with a flashback to the mentality I had known in my early years in Northern Ireland. Thus, he struck a familiar chord when he reminded me a little too often to be careful to save electricity.

'Don't forget to make out zee light,' he had warned. My newly acquired German helped me replace his 'make' with 'put' and I understood. Mutti, on the other hand, had learnt English as a hobby and taken no serious interest in it. As a result, communication with her was more of a challenge and one particular incident proved the point. In the cellar of our building of five apartments there were piles of short timber offcuts used to fuel the wood burning furnace in winter. Along with these, shelves of preserved fruits and vegetables with bins of potatoes and onions that had been harvested from the summer garden were stored. One day Mutti sent me down to the cellar with a slowly enunciated request,

'Please bring me some bread.' I wondered at this, for I had never seen bread in the cellar. Nonetheless, I scoured the basement space for a loaf but there was none. Returning to her apartment empty-handed, I confessed my lack of success while she insisted that the bread was indeed down there. Duly chastened, I was about to make a second trip down when Papa, on his way home from work, met me in the hallway.

'Going out, Sweetie?' he smiled with genuine interest.

'No, I'm on my way to the cellar to collect some bread for Mutti,' I informed him.

'Bread, from the cellar?' he queried incredulously. 'But, we don't keep bread in the cellar.' With that he opened the door to his apartment and called to his wife in German:

'What did you want from the cellar?'

'Brette,' she said with growing impatience.

'And why did you send for bread? "Wood" is the word for what you want, not "bread". No wonder Sweetie here is puzzled!' With that clarification it was easy to run downstairs and avail myself of an armful of short timber offcuts from the stack. In all of this, nothing was wasted for out of the confusion I learned a new German word, though admittedly, it would not be quite as useful as bread!

It was early in our honeymoon year when John began to realise the extent of my visual problem. When he encouraged me to sing from the German hymnbook, I was unable to read the text.

'It'll help you learn the language,' he urged.

'But I can't see it,' I objected.

'Of course you can see it, just hold it closer,' he insisted. I admit his lack of understanding offended me and my failure to comply annoyed him. Added to this was his obvious disappointment, confessed in a moment of candour.

'You know, I had thought you were a reader but I don't see you with any books,' he had sighed. Without expressing it, I acknowledged the truth to myself that we did not really know one another well and a courtship of separation, sustained by a weekly exchange of letters alone, had not been ideal. Distance had robbed us of the opportunity to learn to truly know each other. Added to this was the challenge of dealing with my disability, now fully realised, and what it might mean for us as a couple. Granted, this could only be fully known as we encountered the daily experiences of life delivered to us by an untried future.

As it was, uncertainty began to claim my peace of mind. The darkest stretch in my living patchwork was real enough but was it about to overshadow the bright fabric of recent joys? Would I be robbed of new found happiness or would there be a way forward? In my view, the key lay with John. Would he be able to accept my legal blindness? Would he be able to see past my disability to value the person I was? Though love motivated me to please John in whatever way I could, I did not think my acceptance with him lay in 'trying harder' in order to gain his approval. I considered this a futile goal with little to indicate it could ever be reached in any consistent way. I thought it better to live by my own standards, as I always had, believing my values were sound. In terms of values, John and I held much in common. Our mutual choice to live for God was paramount and it gave us a level playing field for working out the rest of life.

As far as the value I saw in myself was concerned, that was not in question. I never had measured my worth against the opinions of other people so, poor vision or no, I felt myself to be as worthwhile as anyone else. This was probably because my sense of worth did not rest in what I could or could not do, but in who I was. There was an early secret to this for, beyond belonging to my parents, I considered myself a daughter of God and had done so for as long as I could remember. No one had told me this, I just knew it to be true and the knowledge provided me with a kind of privileged status. Later learning from Scripture only served to confirm this. It preserved me from the secular notion that I needed to depend on other people's approbation alongside a positive self-assessment, to carve out a healthy self-image. I admit that sometimes I lost sight of the firm foundation I had chosen, especially when it came to significant human relationships. This happened when I knew I could see a lot less than John realised, and fear of a loss of status in his eyes posed a threat to me. It was, of course, a threat to my self-esteem which

I later recognised as being different from personal worth. I knew it usually took some time for the labile emotions associated with a threat to self-esteem to stabilise and allow me to reaffirm the stable basis of my personal worth. I discovered that under an emotional attack, self-esteem may suffer from time to time until personal worth reasserts itself and overcomes the hurt.

It concerned me that without the foundation on which I depended as a basis for personal worth, I could easily try to build my worth on pride. Of course, one must sit on a high horse to exercise pride and I had seen it done effectively on many occasions with the skilful use of self-defence. Should I adopt this approach, I could imagine myself believing largely in my own capacities to establish personal worth. When under a perceived threat, for instance, I could find emotional stability again with the aid of self-defence, and this would protect me from hurt and guilt. It did sound plausible, but there was a major risk and a price to pay, for pride is known to damage relationships. The kind of protection it provided depended on high levels of social exclusiveness at worst, or on strict selectivity at best. This is because it is grounded in distrust and easily develops into hostility. Metaphorically, distrust builds walls between people and these are certainly effective against emotional hurt. The trouble is it also works against friendship and intimacy. The gentle vulnerability that needs no barriers, but makes a person welcome and their company desirable, eludes the proud because it only belongs to the humble who accept other people in an environment of trust. I had grown up with consistent exposure to the skilful use of pride and it would have been easy to draw on its *modus operandi* to survive in my relationship with John. Survival alone is a long way from marital bliss and it would mean living by the rules of pride, that is, never admit to being in the wrong; when criticised, defend; reveal as little as you can about your opinions and feelings, then you cannot be judged by them; project an ideal image of yourself rather than the flawed reality; when scrutiny threatens, close down because opening up to people can be dangerous. Dare I choose the humbler route with its potential to leave me vulnerable to hurt, should I be criticised? Could I cope with a demolished self-esteem? I cringed at the thought.

As it turned out, John was doing his own thinking about the future of our marriage. He had been shaped to a degree by his experiences near the end of the Second World War. As a five year-old refugee in flight from Western Prussia before the Red Army's westward advance, he was thrust into a very early adulthood. In the absence of his father, he bore responsibility for the care and safety of his toddler brother and baby sister while their mother queued for hours for a daily ration of milk and bread. As enemy aircraft flew overhead discharging their deadly cargo, their mother offered the only protection she had. Kneeling on the ground, she gathered her three small children close to her. Then she spread her body over them as a human shield. While she prayed, 'God spare us', a keen need to protect, that would remain with him for the rest of his life, was implanted in John. It was this keen sense of protection that strengthened John's commitment to care for me as he realised the severity of my visual disability. Though occasionally 'parented' by him, I never doubted his devotion to me, his respect or his pride in me as I exercised my abilities to our mutual benefit. I was never demeaned nor diminished in public or in private by John who truly loved and valued me. Thus he became my defender, set on encouraging my further development in the ways I chose to grow and supporting my every decision for the good.

CHAPTER 7

To Add or not to Add

Like all good things, honeymoons come to an end and life in the real world begins anew. Our year in Europe finished with Christmas. It was a delightful season of novel treats, marzipan, gifts and special meals, even if the main event for most took place on Christmas Eve. Still, there was an advantage to this custom, for it left families free to attend church on Christmas Day and to feast on the abundance of musical programs on offer. Christmas over and hugs exchanged with smiles and tears, we farewelled friends and family, departing Europe by train on the first day of the New Year. John's parents were naturally sad to see us go, but it was clear to us that our future lay on the other side of the world. We spent a happy fortnight with my grandmother in England visiting more family and friends before setting sail again for Australia. This time the voyage lasted three weeks and the sea was exceptionally calm. As a rule, I would not be susceptible to motion sickness under these conditions, but this time I was. With persistent nausea ailing me, I spent the greater part of most days lying listlessly on my bunk, refusing food and harbouring the strong suspicion I was pregnant.

After a slow trip through the Suez Canal and a one-day stop in Sri Lanka, Fremantle was the harbour to welcome us home. Like a grim spectre rising up to greet me, I remembered landing at this port ten years before. I recalled my fear of the unknown and the homesickness that accompanied our first arrival. This time, however, things were different and, energised by excitement I shot a directive at John,

'Look down there on the quay, Honey. Can you see the family waiting for us?'

'Yes, indeed. Your Dad and Mum are in the middle of the group and everyone is waving to us.' Warm hugs enveloped us and our luggage was lifted by strong young hands and carried to the waiting cars. A year had been a long time.

During our absence in Europe, Dad had bought us a near new car at a very good price with the money I had saved in New Zealand. With this and a bit more shopping, we were almost ready to travel east. John had been offered a post in Victoria and again, it was going to be difficult to leave family—mine this time. We would have a few weeks together in the sunny west before beginning the 3,400 kilometre trip. In order to preserve its good condition, we avoided driving our car on the 1,670 kilometre length of unsealed road that stretched from Norseman to Port Augusta. Though boasting the descriptor 'highway' it was the only road across the desert and its unforgiving surface was pitted with gaping potholes. These were deceptively hidden from view under a camouflage of fine bulldust, and for the inexperienced, this usually meant falling up to the axle into deep depressions. Instead of risking this and the damage it might cause, we loaded our car onto a train and travelled the distance in comfort. The train was well equipped with sleeping berths and a dining car where waiters took our orders and served us formal meals. It was decidedly the better option.

'I won't mind driving the last part of the journey,' mused John. 'A tar-sealed road will be easy on the car as we travel from Adelaide to Melbourne.'

Our first assignment was in the city of Melbourne and John was to work with five other young ministers under the direction of a senior evangelist. He was also to pastor one of the smaller city churches with its trans-European congregation. There were many German immigrants in the area and our language skills were helpful in communicating with them. Since ships had begun to give way to planes as a means of passenger transport between Europe and Australia, adventurous youth were on the move. Several from Germany, Austria and Switzerland exploring the world with a backpack, came to our little church and stayed, enlarging its congregation appreciably. Our primary concern on arriving in Melbourne was to find accommodation,

'Where do you think they'll house us?' I wanted to know and John's answer was realistic,

'Somewhere humble I should think.' Humble it was, consisting of one half of an old house that had been converted into two apartments. If not plush, it was adequate with a kitchen, bathroom, bedroom, and an all-purpose living room. A back veranda had been covered in to create an extra room and this became John's study. The apartment was already furnished with the basics and two small garden plots—one at the front, the other at the rear completed the dwelling. A major advantage turned out to be its location. Apart from its proximity to shops, a private hospital with a new maternity wing stood at the corner of our street. A few weeks after moving in I made an appointment for a check-up there and was left with no surprises.

'You're three months pregnant,' advised the obstetrician. In a month I would turn twenty five and I was in top condition, fully fit, thoroughly healthy and expecting a baby with a due arrival date in late September. I was delighted! My pregnancy confirmed, the notion of living patchwork fired my imagination.

Anne of Green Gables would have found a 'kindred spirit' in me for I loved to dream. It was a way of transforming the ordinary into the ideal with a temptation to believe in its reality. Anne would say it is people of imagination who excel at this. So I began to dream of a beautiful vision in pink. I saw myself sitting out on a tartan rug under a cherry blossom tree in spring, in the privacy of a well-kept garden (even if the actual was small and scruffy with no cherry tree). Beside me was a white bassinet lined with delicate pastel pink and trimmed with satin ribbon. Fully contented and peacefully asleep in a rose embroidered bonnet and dress lay my precious baby girl.

The months passed and September came, and with it, the birth of my son. With his arrival I concluded that far from helping us build an ideal picture, imagination must be ours to protect us from the ruthlessness of reality. If I had expected a slumbering vision in pink, or any colour for that matter, it was not visible to me. In fact, baby David was given to very little sleep preferring to holler with hunger most of the time, especially at night. His appetite was voracious. He would feed till satiated, take a short nap and then wake up roaring with hunger once again. Had we waited out the standard four hour interval between feeds recommended at the baby clinic, it would have rendered John and me a couple of nervous wrecks. We grabbed at the notion of feeding on demand not minding the intervals and this became our solution. David had been born long and slender with soft baby skin that hung loosely from his upper arms and thighs. While other babies were filled out with adequate flesh at birth, it took little David three months to catch up on the condition of his peers. In the meantime, sleep was a luxury forfeited by all except David, who made up for his nights of noisy complaint with catnaps during the day. If babies have a motto, David's was 'be alert'.

While other babies lay in prams, strollers or bassinets contentedly cooing, David, at a few months old, struggled against gravity in an attempt to sit up. Unable as yet to master this of his own accord, he favoured being propped with his back against his father's chest for support to access an unobstructed view. In this way, he could survey the world around him and was content.

Just how much he could see of the world around him was a constant question in our minds. Were his two clear blue eyes, focussed so steadily on distant objects fully sighted, or were they flawed like my own? A merciful Providence supplied the answer. Beach lovers by inclination, we were walking along a sandy edge of the Pacific Ocean one fine day looking for shells to share with our baby boy. An early talker with an ever increasing vocabulary, David looked along the beach from his perch on his father's shoulders and pointed, crying,

'Awsey! Awsey!'

'Can you see a horse, Honey?' I enquired of John, hope springing in my heart.

'No, I can't,' he replied with a slow shake of his head, and then, 'O yes, I believe there is a horse but it's a long way off.' I took David in my arms and hugged him tight as tears of joy pricked my eyes and wet my face,

'Thank you Lord, thank you!' I choked as I recognised the answer to my prayers and realised that David's life would not be blighted with the malady that marked my own. He would be able to see like other fully sighted children and would have no visual difficulties at school. Any profession he chose would be open to him. He could even be a brain surgeon, I inwardly sighed, my imagination soaring to the greatest conjecture possible once again.

If not limited eyesight, David was born with a particular

challenge. It was not a challenge to the boy himself but to me, and it would test my equanimity like no other. He was incredibly mobile, possessing higher than usual energy levels and in this, he was very like his father. In observing his constant activity, well-meaning friends would advise,

'Your child is so restless he probably has ADD (Attention Deficit Disorder).' A neighbour with a placid, plump little girl seated quietly at her feet once remarked,

'David never sits still so perhaps you should get him tested.' I knew my son was highly active and was often diagnosed as 'hyper' by local purveyors of homespun remedies. I also knew there was no pathology in his high levels of activity because he could also sit quietly for an hour or more, engrossed in a toy or book that had captured his interest and apply exceptional powers of concentration to it. His high levels of mobility meant he was simply up and off and out of sight before I could discover his intention. Due to my visual limitation, at five metres distance from me, I had no idea where he was. Though I had carefully taught him to listen for my voice and to come when I called, he was often distracted or too far away to hear me. Thus, during David's early years we were well known to the police wherever we happened to live. Several times I ran, heart in mouth, to the local police station to report my missing child. Always he would be there, sitting up on the counter or in a chair rewarded for his disappearance with a banana or a lollipop. Fear of being lost did not deter David from these early escapades. I doubt he ever felt he was lost nor do I think it occurred to him to be frightened. But then, given my own orientation to frightening childhood experiences, he did come by that trait honestly. On the other hand, though he was always happy to see me when I appeared, David was equally happy in the company of the constable. I thanked God so often for his rescue and for the kindly, wholesome people who had found him and taken him to safety.

As far as the genetic transmission of my poor vision was concerned, there was little to go by at the time and being convinced that David's sight was unimpaired, I was keen to have another baby. Having grown up with no siblings of my own, the only child in me shrank from leaving David to the same lonely fate. I wanted him to grow up with someone who would share childhood experiences with him. I hoped for two children who could be constant companions because they would not be alone.

'Let them be born as close together as you can,' was the conventional wisdom of the day, 'that way, they'll go through the same life stages together and will more likely be close friends.' Chances were, I would have another child like David but I did not stop to question my capacity to manage two like him. My desire to provide David with the sibling I never had, overcame any misgivings that might have lingered in my mind. Before taking this step, however, I took the opportunity to reflect on my attitude to life, weighing both positive and negative aspects. Admittedly, with my sanguine nature, I gave more weight to the positive and began to consider scraps in living patchwork as dark, only when I could do nothing to lighten them. I decided that dark belonged to the things I could not change or find a way to accommodate. These were great immovable obstacles blocking progress towards a goal. There was no denying that the large dark presence of low vision in my living patchwork affected all I did but the many bright pieces that came together to ensure my living well were not to be ignored. As for lesser dark fragments, there were plenty of areas in my living patchwork where I could find a way around the difficulty they posed and this made me resolute and determined not to let anything stand in my way that could be overcome. With this optimistic mindset, life had good prospects and I looked forward to having another child.

In those days it was said that two years between births was about the right interval. It gave enough space to gather strength for another pregnancy and sufficient time to toilet train the older child. Because disposable nappies were yet to find their way into common use in Australia, toilet training was a major focus. Daily, backyard clotheslines sported up to a dozen snow-white flannel or towelling nappies. This was evidence that there was a baby in the house. If the count was twice the expected number, however, it was assumed that, unless there were twins involved, the occupants had not quite managed to get the interval right and had two babies in nappies at the same time. By the time David was two and a bit we had mastered the art of toilet training with the very occasional mishap. If there was a mishap, and lest my toddler be embarrassed by the event, I would reassure him gently with,

'Never mind Darling, it's only an accident, you couldn't help it,' Then one day, after some cows had strayed into our next door neighbour's back yard and left a sizeable deposit on the lawn, David climbed over the fence to visit the neighbour who was hanging washing on the clothesline. Suddenly he spied the evidence of the cows' visit and approaching our neighbour cautiously, pointed at the cow dung. Speaking with great compassion, he consoled,

'Nevamine Mitheth Smif, sonie an assiden. You coon hep it.' I arrived in time to find Mrs Smith rocking with laughter and a concerned David looking on.

As it was, the favoured two year interval between births eluded us. Five months too early, I found myself with the all too familiar symptoms of pregnancy. Envisioning a future with copious clotheslines of daily laundry, I could hear Mother's casual comment sounding in my ears,

'The women in our family are particularly fertile. Nobody has trouble conceiving.' David was just one year old and my imagination was still capable of conjuring up a vision in pink. So I anticipated the coming of the little girl I knew would be next to grace our home, providing us with the popular blend known as 'a pigeon pair.'

CHAPTER 8

To Hold or not to Hold

Nineteen months after David's birth, chubby, contented Charlie dropped into our lives to complete our family unit. No longer fully convinced about the vision in pink, I had made six small gender-neutral nighties in anticipation of his arrival. These, added to a pile of newborn clothes in good condition inherited from David, augmented his wardrobe nicely. In this way, Charlie was rendered an adequately, if inexpensively, attired little boy.

If David was active, prone to wakefulness and often restless, Charlie was quite the opposite. During the day he would happily lie down, sleep five hours at a time in his pram, bassinet, or even in my arms, and had no trouble sleeping through the night. A baby who wanted to be cuddled was a new experience for me and I revelled in the closeness and affection he brought. As babies go, the contrast between the two was remarkable. If I parked David somewhere in his pram, I could only leave him briefly before a fellow shopper would tap me on the shoulder with the warning,

'I think your baby's in trouble.' Hurrying back, I would find he had partially freed himself from his safety straps, was hanging suspended upside down over the side of the pram and was loudly protesting his predicament. Charlie, on the other hand, could see little sense in this activity, preferring to sit quietly in the pram smiling at passers-by for however long it took for me to come and move him on. Such convenient conditions have a habit of changing, however, and by the time Charlie had begun to walk we were living in a house with no front fence. If we went out into the garden and Charlie was more than five metres away from me, I knew I would not be able to see him. This led me to take desperate measures to secure his safety. Strapping a toddler harness to his little body, I attached a rope of several metres to the back of it. This done, I tied the other end to the base of the rotary clothesline. The rope allowed him scope to run up the side of the house from back to front on lawn, but stopped him at the curb before he could go on the road. The strategy was ingenious, unpopular, and a great source of frustration for Charlie who never did work out what was impeding his carefree progress. As they grew, personality differences continued to characterise the two. It could be assumed that conflict would be inevitable between the go-getter type-A David and the laid-back type-B Charlie, while their growing dissimilarities would lead to their drifting apart. Surprisingly, this did not happen. The bond I had hoped would be theirs did develop, and it remained important to them both for the years to come.

Because David's sight had proved to be unimpaired, in Charlie's case we had relaxed our vigilant observation to some extent. At least, we were not as anxious to test his vision. To that point in time there was no evidence that my condition was genetically transmitted so we took it for granted there would be no problem. However, living patchwork is fraught with the unexpected as dark pieces come uninvited and unplanned to join the crazy pattern of our lives. So it was that one day, while we were playing indoors with toy cranes, dump trucks and bulldozers, a natural opportunity arose to test Charlie's vision, just to be sure all was well. Making a game of it, I sent the boys into the hallway. Next, I stowed a red bulldozer under a high-legged chair in a corner of the living room. Then, I brought the boys into the room, one at a time, and asked them to locate the bulldozer. David was first to enter. Immediately, he spotted the toy and, with a whoop of triumph, ran to retrieve it. Soon it was Charlie's turn and he entered with equal enthusiasm. Standing in the middle of the floor he looked in every direction, but to no avail. He could not see the toy anywhere. Wanting to help, David ran over and grabbing Charlie by the hand led him to the relevant corner. When they had reached a spot, about a metre from the toy, Charlie exclaimed: 'Oh, der 'tiz Davie!' and he scooped it up possessively in his chubby little hands.

The incident revived an almost forgotten memory for me. Again I saw my father and a corgi cardboard box on a country lane in County Down. I knew this memory would portend a ceaseless struggle for my son and I felt the pain. Dismayed and broken by self-reproach, I fled the room leaving the boys to their toys.

No! I silently screamed amidst my tears whilst I pointed an accusing finger at God. 'You heard my prayers for David and made sure your protective hand was over his vision, but what about Charlie? Why haven't you given him the same chance? It doesn't matter about me! I've made it through life thus far and can manage for the rest, but was it necessary for this child to be so blighted? It isn't fair!' In my distress I could not understand why this had happened, but I knew the problem had come from me. Despite the fact I had not chosen it for Charlie, I keenly felt responsible for his plight and guilt weighed heavily on me. I had done this to him and could see no way to fix it. It was one thing to manage the mysterious condition in my own life, but now it was clear it could be passed on to my offspring through my DNA. At this new realisation, I gritted my teeth and vowed I would bring no more children into this world.

Knowing from my own experience the struggle that lay ahead for Charlie, this became a highly unwelcome part of my living patchwork and I resented it deeply,
    'Well, that's just it,' I cynically declared to the ceiling. 'Life offers no one a free hand to choose the pieces that go to make up the crazy patchwork life they must live. If I could choose, this patch would not be in Charlie's life at all!' But I could not choose no matter how much I wished it. There was a shred of consolation, though, in that Charlie did have a precedent in me. He could see how I coped regardless of the obstacles. This could be of help to him in carving out his future. As a child, there had been plenty of pity, some sympathy and a degree of empathy for my disability. Nonetheless, no one else known to me had gone before to set a pattern for how to live as normal a life as possible with this kind of handicap. Yet, I was managing somehow and now, as a mother, I would need to negotiate again the same familiar dark patch as it stretched its ugly influence over Charlie's life. I hoped that in having travelled the same road, I might be of some help to my boy. Taking the words from my angry prayer,
    'I've made it through life thus far and can manage for the rest,' I determined to share with Charlie whatever coping skills I had gained. I would support him in practical ways and endeavour to build his resilience with positive emotional support, but I would not mollycoddle him. He would have to face obstacles and overcome them. Where it was needed, I would show him how I managed the challenges of low vision and encourage him to rise to meet them too.
    In the process, I was not about to cast God off as malevolent

or redundant. I knew He was behind everything good in our world and was not responsible for its evils. Deprived already of normal vision, I would not by poor example, deprive Charlie of faith as well, nor of the present and future promises faith provided. Although I was yet to arrive at some answers to difficult questions that tested my own faith, I firmly believed that, one day, we would both be able to see as well as everyone else even if it meant waiting for a new world order. In the meantime, if Charlie chose to put his trust in God, He would help him manage life.

Whether in his very early years David understood Charlie's need or not was uncertain, but he often met it anyway by calling Charlie to come with him, wherever they were going, so they could find their way together. As David grew in age and understanding, both Charlie and I increasingly depended on him to cross roads, read signs and street names, see bus numbers and make out their destinations. In this way his eyes served the three of us as we found our way about in a potentially dangerous world. As for David, he seemed to view this as a vote of confidence and showed no signs of resenting it. It was fortunate indeed for us that along with his quick, alert mind, David also possessed a good deal of compassion. This prevented him from growing impatient with us or refusing to be helpful.

As a family, the values we espoused were thoroughly Christian. We tended to live above the world of heartless competition with its 'me-first' orientation, its focus on getting ahead at the expense of others and its noticeable lack of selfless love.

'It's God first, others next and self, last,' John would repeat and it made for personal peace and contentment in our lives. David and Charlie were immersed in this world view and perhaps it is why they knew the value of co-operation and mutual consideration. Above all, they learned not to take themselves too seriously. Nonetheless, while holding a set of values is one thing, living by them consistently is quite another. So, like any other Christian family we had our imperfections. We had spats and disagreements, a testing of the parameters and a challenging of the boundaries, some resentments and the occasional rebellion. We also had the underpinnings of the love that comes from God and found it to have an unrivalled quality. This is what held us together in relative harmony.

The child-raising trend of the time included conflict resolution by democratic negotiation.

'Teach them to discuss their differences and resolve issues with a win-win outcome,' it said. In our case this simply did not work. Attempts at negotiation deteriorated into heated arguments with exchanges of blame like:

'He took mine!'

'No, I didn't, it's mine. He lost his!' I concluded that whoever wrote those books had never tried to raise youngsters. Furthermore, if adult leaders of nations could not solve their problems through democratic negotiation, what hope did children have? I decided my children needed the rule of law clearly defined by someone in charge—me. In the end we took a short, mostly effective route to discipline. It included confinement to the bedroom for misdemeanours for a period of time. This frustrated David but it gave Charlie time to finish his jigsaw puzzle! It also gave opportunity for reform that lasted for a while at least. We also imposed sanctions for noncompliance which reduced the delivery and consumption of treats for a day or two. Neither boy cared for this one. When all else failed, we waved a wooden spoon over their heads threatening to use it, after a count of three, if we were not being heeded. Thankfully, we rarely passed two before they capitulated and complied with our directives. In general, and in harmony with the times, we believed that children must learn to obey their parents and a smack or two for flagrant violation of the parental will was appropriate.

In our house, a remnant of the democratic negotiation model did survive. This was probably due to its empowering appeal and evident success. It was the family council. It consisted of a collaborative effort at planning family events including holidays, outings and recreational activities at home and beyond. There was also the inevitable list of household chores to be allocated. Fortunately, the boys saw logic in the principle of work before play, though they needed a periodic reminder that agreement with a principle was one thing, while putting it into practice was quite another. Seizing an opportunity to down tools, Charlie was usually first to arrive and claim a chair at the family council. David, on the other hand, began early to develop his father's strong work ethic and would head off to complete his chores immediately discussion ended. Charlie was less motivated, preferring to lie on his back on the grass to weeding his patch of garden. Until caught out idling, he could make many an animal shape, person or edifice out of the cloud formations that floated overhead. In this respect, no allowances were made for Charlie's low vision. The childhood expectations placed on him to produce results from an assigned task were just as high as they had been for me at the same age. In this way Charlie ultimately developed an adequate work ethic and managed to live a near normal life.

A further aspect to our family culture was spontaneous physical contact. Without thinking much about it, the two little boys would climb up and sprawl across their father's chest or snuggle up close to him for story time. Wrestling began at the toddler stage with John holding both boys at bay with one hand in an easy win. As time went by, however, the win became harder to achieve and the match would often end in a giggling heap of masculine humanity crumpled on the floor. Ultimately, John confessed,

'Together, they're too strong for me now. I'm not able to overpower them anymore.' From then on wrestling was limited to two competitors only until one day, whilst in a match with Charlie, David put his foot through the panelling of an internal timber door. Because of this, the place for wrestling was strictly limited to outdoors until the boys reached their late teens when the activity died a natural death.

Physical contact was also a good salve for problems at primary school. I was usually at home when school finished and available to deal with crises. I could receive one or other of the boys into my arms and onto my lap if need be. This seemed to help as they debriefed on a classroom injustice or lamented a social defeat on a playground that doubled as a warzone. For the most part Charlie, who was good at maths, kept bullies at bay by trading an offer to do their homework for a guarantee of physical safety. It was not so easy for David who, desperately wanting acceptance, sometimes found himself friendless in an alien culture. This was most apparent when he had just changed countries, cultures and classrooms and was now in his final year of primary school. Not given to tears, he carried his sadness on his drooping shoulders and wore it etched on his unhappy face. On an otherwise sunny afternoon he once pushed his way slowly in through the front door of our home. I handed him the customary glass of fruit juice and asked the standard question,

'How was school today son?' The picture of misery, he lifted his eyes to mine and I could sense his abject loneliness. 'Come to me,' I gently coaxed. He sank wordlessly onto my lap and allowed his tears to flow. It was a rare moment of healing. As a family, we never did force an end to physical contact at any time and continued to greet and acknowledge one another with hugs and kisses indefinitely.

When it dawned on us that Charlie had low vision, we thought the expert opinion of an eye specialist timely. Unfortunately, the condition was so rare that it was relatively unknown, even within the profession. As a consequence, Charlie's better eye was patched over with a light adhesive tape and he was left to manage with only the eye of lesser sight. With this treatment, it was thought his vision in the uncovered eye would improve to equal the strength of his better eye. It was an exercise in futility and no good resulted from it. I was angry at myself for my lack of assertiveness in allowing this approach. Nonetheless, a dubious benefit did come from it. Charlie and David had collected a bundle of small magazines from church containing stories for children. Seeing we had read them all, I suggested we go down to the city where we could share them by handing them out to other children who might be passing by. The boys were enthusiastic at the notion and happily set about the task. On the day, Charlie was wearing his eye patch and it caused a bit of misunderstanding. I positioned myself at a distance from the boys and let them distribute the magazines. I was too far from them, however, to be able to see exactly what was happening. Consequently, when we arrived home, I was alarmed to discover Charlie had a pocketful of unsolicited donations that added up to a tidy sum! We concluded that people observing Charlie's eye patch must have thought we were collecting for disadvantaged children. The money gave us the extra duty of seeing that such a cause did in fact receive the cash gathered in Charlie's pocket.

There were times, however, when the world was against Charlie and his eye patch. Our home was located on a moderate hill opposite a primary school. Wearing his eye patch, four year old Charlie would careen downhill on his tricycle on the footpath that ran past our house. Once he ploughed headlong into a group of youngsters on their way home from school. Of course the children protested volubly, and for very good reason. Undaunted, Charlie argued back as to who had right of way. In the end, it was left to the respective fathers to sort the problem out and John encouraged the offending Charlie to apologise. He just had not seen the other children. Thus the unwanted scrap, so familiar to me, began to spread its dark hue over Charlie's life. From then until the eye patch was discarded, his tricycle was towed up and down the footpath on a rope pulled by John, while Charlie steered irrelevantly and was no longer a rider of independent will. I knew his temporary compliance would not last and Charlie would eventually learn to seek independence as diligently as I had done.

Along with the joys of child-raising, the child within me was beginning to crave some new dimensions to life. Gone were the halcyon days of post-war simplicity when self-actualisation for women amounted to raising a family, growing a vegetable garden, sewing, knitting and keeping house. Important as those activities were, they started to lose their value as baby-boomer women graduated with affordable university degrees and entered the workforce in appreciable numbers. At the same time, married women in their thirties and forties caught the trend and headed back to the lecture theatre driven by the desire to develop a new career. For them, the lure of a second income, complete with discretionary spending money of their own, was equally compelling. Many husbands appreciated the benefits of this extra income, but for those who did not, conflict gnawed at their marital peace. The old axiom: 'Where there is wealth, there is power' changed the leadership dynamic in several homes as women began to take hold of their share of family government and assume greater authority. This shift anticipated that men would assume more responsibility for childcare and housework, but the outcome was debatable. Apart from a minority, men had not been educated in the skills of homemaking. Thus, numbers of women found they were frustrated and fatigued as they tried to shoulder the increased load. For some the very definition of 'home' changed. No longer was it a sanctuary where the family could retire to a safe haven at the end of the day and find a freshly cooked meal waiting for them. Instead, it became a kind of way station where people passed each other *en route* to somewhere else. Such momentous domestic change contributed to casualties in the married sector and instances of divorce increased. To describe the developing situation, terms like 'hassle,' 'stress' and 'pressure' became common household words. A married friend of mine had two sons and a busy medical practice. As we chatted one day she quipped,

'It's not a husband I need, it's a wife.' Her sentiment spoke for many.

CHAPTER 9

To Go or not to Go

To be honest, the new dimension I sought was much more modest than that of my medical friend. John was strongly career oriented with little or no time to spend on housework. As tradition would have it, he mowed the lawns, washed the car and spent time with the boys, playing games and building model planes and boats. Mine was the pivotal presence—the centre around which home in all its aspects revolved. It was my role to provide a clean, tidy house where the family could comfortably relax together. Washing and ironing kept up to date with regular wholesome meals and a productive vegetable garden were part of the package. Much as I wanted to register in a course of study, I had no problem in being committed to this domestic mould. On the other hand, John had spent five years as a part-time student preparing for a Batchelor of Divinity degree from London University and had recently completed it with honours. He had thanked me on several occasions for my patience while he spent so much time in study,

'Had you not supported and encouraged me over the years, I wouldn't have been able to get this degree,' he confessed with a grateful smile. Seizing the opportunity I replied,

'Actually, I'd like to take a course of study myself.'

'Splendid idea,' John agreed and with the mentality of the times he added,

'Do you think you'll be able to manage it given your time commitment to the boys and me as well as the running of the house?' In unspoken answer, I was determined to manage it. It was a coveted piece I longed to include in my living patchwork. It would be a contrast to the many scraps that randomly happened along, whether I wanted to work them into the design of my life or not. It would be a chosen piece and I was not about to let it go,

'I was thinking of taking a unit in German,' I continued, 'I do have a head start with the year we spent in Germany and the night school classes I took there—such as they were. It would be good to capitalise on this and get some academic credit into the bargain. It's only one unit.' With John convinced and with no further ado, I enrolled as a distance student at University in a terminal unit, German 1B.

This was my bright new patch squeezed in between washing floors, clothes and dishes, shopping, cooking, mending, ironing and gardening as well as story-time and more with the boys. I was fortunate in that David was already in grade one at school and Charlie played contentedly with the neighbourhood children in their backyard or ours. This was my window of opportunity for study and I grabbed it. Although the unit was offered as a distance option, students were required to physically attend a two week residential school on campus each year. It was here that I met Gillian, mother of two, who was also enrolled in German 1B. Gillian watched me read in class, and saw how closely I held the text to my eyes,

'Excuse me,' she ventured, 'I'm Gillian and I hope you don't mind my commenting but I see you read by holding the text very close. You see, my second child has albinism. Her vision is severely compromised by the condition and I'm anxious to learn how others cope with this limitation. Please come, I'd like you to meet my family.' We approached a white Ferrari parked by the curb. A fine looking bearded man stepped out trailing a six year old boy and a girl of four. The girl had strikingly white hair and skin and, though it was winter, her eyes were shaded with sunglasses. Confident and assertive, the children smiled and waved a brief, 'hello' before bounding off to play on the university lawn. When they were out of earshot, Gillian introduced me to her husband Peter, a medical specialist with a noticeably cool, aloof air,

'Carole is in the German class with me. I wanted you to meet her because she has similar visual challenges to Clara,' Gillian explained. Peter's interest sharpened quickly and he turned to me:

'How has this affected your daily life, especially your school years? You're in a study program at the moment, so can you read normal print? How about driving, do you have a licence?' I answered his questions as best I could, assuring him poor eyesight did not have to greatly limit his daughter's life. There would be many things she would be able to do where she could depend on faculties beyond sight.

'Tell you what,' he offered. 'I'm leaving in two weeks for a medical conference in Germany and I'd be happy to bring you back a large-print version of the texts for the unit you and Gillian are taking. Might that help?' In those days when portable reading aids were limited to spectacles with strong lenses and handheld magnifiers, this was a wonderful offer. True to his word, Peter brought the books back to Australia and Gillian delivered them to me in good time to be useful for study. The gesture represented a small luminous swatch designed to lighten my living patchwork. I was deeply grateful and glad to add it to the whole.

Given my background in German the unit was easy and,

breezing through, I collected a high distinction in the final exam. For the following year, a German 1B student achieving an HD was permitted to take a giant leap up to enrol in German 2A. A few weeks into this unit and I began to fall behind. I could see it was going to take more time than I had to give, and if I were to continue, home and family would suffer. Reluctantly, I took the only option open to me and pulled out at the end of the first term. I told myself I was only waiting for a more favourable moment when I could take it up again. As a child, however, I had not been permitted to pull out of anything, and doing so now did not sit well with me. Nor did it please John who was visibly disappointed at my decision. As I confronted it, the action made me feel a failure as despondency, and finally depression, set in. I had not realised how much of an aspiration further study had become. It was not just a hobby after all. It was a goal—a stepping stone to something more and I knew it.

Time passed but time did not heal for I was still harbouring hopes of a more fulfilling future. Eventually, early November came and we woke as usual to a warm spring day. Little did we realise this would be the day our lives would change forever. It started in an ordinary way with the tolling of the school bell and David's departure. Not for the first time, Charlie stood forlornly at the flyscreen door watching his brother run down the road to the pedestrian crossing, over the road and into school. Today would be different. An intentional lean on the door and it sprang open again under Charlie's weight. The temptation to follow David was too great to resist, so out through the door barefoot, with remnants of breakfast cereal clinging to his face and his hair uncombed, Charlie headed for school. Shrewd beyond his years, he had learned that acceptable behaviour brings rewards. He also knew where grade one met and silently he inched his way into the classroom to slide into a vacant desk near the door. His plan was to spend the morning there in quiet inclusion. Meanwhile, I was searching the house and garden for him when a neighbour called to me,

'Looking for Charlie? I think he went to school after David—might still be down there.' Relieved and amused, I ran over the crossing to retrieve my wandering boy from the grade one classroom. Before reaching it, however, I met the kindly teacher, Mrs Coe, in the corridor leading the ill-groomed, unshod Charlie by the hand,

'Charlie came to visit us this morning and it was very nice to see him,' smiled the thoughtful Mrs Coe. 'He's been to school and he's ready to go home now,' she nodded.

'But I want to stay!' cried the small intruder.

'You will be able to stay when you wash your face, comb your hair and have a uniform with shoes to wear—just like David,' I countered. Satisfied, a subdued Charlie walked home with me without complaint, but with my promise of a swim in the university pool as compensation. I could offer nothing better because both boys were lovers of water. David would throw caution to the wind, and running into the pool's enclosure head straight for the diving board. Running along its full length, he would jump off the end into the pool without stopping for breath. Charlie, who was a good deal shorter than David would cautiously descend the steps into the one metre end wearing inflatable floats. With arms outstretched he would call,

'Look at me!' before his head disappeared beneath the water and I would bend low to fish him out.

Living as we did on a compact campus, John's place of work was less than two hundred metres from our house. This meant he and David could come home for lunch at the same time each day.

John was always a fast walker but on this particular day, he came sprinting down the driveway and clattered in through the flyscreen door, his face alight with excitement,

'Guess what Honey?' he panted, 'I've just come from the Principal's office. They're offering me a two year stint in California as an exchange professor on our affiliated campus. Then they want me to stay on in the States, fully sponsored, to complete a doctorate in Old Testament studies! What do you think about that?' Elated, I danced for joy around the living room to the music of little boy laughter.

'Oh wow! What a wonderful opportunity!' I enthused. Living patchwork was coming up with a beautiful piece of delightful design and I was ready for it. Four years before, when we first moved into this rental home, John had offered to paint and wallpaper the interior of the house if the college supplied the materials. I was willing to provide the unskilled labour and in a couple of weeks the job was done. To make it a child-friendly home, we only needed a few pieces of essential furniture. They included a double bedroom suite donated by my parents, two single beds and a chest of drawers made from two wooden crates and covered with gingham cloth for the boys, basic lounge and dining suites that were factory seconds bought at a furniture auction and a fridge and washing machine that had seen better days. Besides this we had two prized possessions. They were a voluminous library and a tape recorder bought in Singapore on our way home from Germany.

When the offer came to go to the United States it did not take long to dispose of our household goods, such as they were, or the collection of second hand toys belonging to the boys. Most of the ride-on items they owned had been donated by someone who had outgrown them or they were cobbled together and painted by my dad using parts from two or three discarded models. It was easy to sell our car and caravan and, apart from the library, to distribute the rest amongst the cash-strapped married students.

Our only family was still in Western Australia and we would be heading east across the Pacific Ocean. To us, our imminent departure heralded an exciting new adventure but to them, it was an unwelcome severance from all they held dear. The small grandchildren they had driven annually 6,800 kilometres to visit would no longer be in the same country. Saying 'goodbye' was not physically possible so we made a cassette tape recording to mail to them. This would enable them to play our farewells as often as they liked. On the recording the boys explained the sequence of our trip to the States. David had memorised the route very well, island by island, and could rattle it off to perfection. Charlie, on the other hand, was dismissive. Going to America was all very well but his recorded words to Grandad and Nanna were a family matter and he wanted to make it clear,

'We're sending you a "pitcher" of David's class. It's a photo. It's all covered in plassick. Don't try to take it off because… because…well, don't finally weck it!' We bid farewell to friends and neighbours—close daily contacts I feared we might never see again. The sad thing about leaving and moving on is that those you leave behind move on too, and itis impossible to wind back the clock and recapture the lost years of the past. Our sojourn in America would last five years. In that time, we and our world would change dramatically. So, shipping our library ahead and leaving nothing in storage, we packed two suitcases with the rest of our earthly belongings and headed for Sydney airport.

CHAPTER 10

To Change or not to Change

In 1974 it was possible to buy one-way economy class tickets that allowed for a single flight with multiple stopovers. This applied to most countries in the Pacific *en route* to a final destination. Provided passengers kept moving in one direction without back-tracking, the fare would be no more than the cost of a direct flight. Inasmuch as tourism was in its infancy in the region, we decided to take full advantage of the option and board a UTA flight in Sydney bound for San Francisco.

'Well David, where do you think our first stop will be?' quizzed John and the answer was immediate,

'New Caledonia, Dad!' Arriving in Noumea, we noticed at once the separation of the French population from the indigenous Melanesians. Integration was not in the national reckoning nor was it sought by either ethnic group. Each was content to live within the confines of its own culture and to mix little with the other. This proved to be a general social rule for several Pacific island nations where more than one ethnic group inhabited a country. As for us, we were fortunate to know a number from various islands who had been students in Australia. This gave us the chance to visit cross-culturally in comfort as we made our way over the vast expansive sea.

After spending Christmas Eve at our first island stop, we arrived next day in Nadi, Fiji in time to enjoy a traditional

Christmas dinner. We ate with our friends, Akanisi and Kalara from a chiefly family. Ushering us into a conventional dwelling or 'bure', Akanisi addressed us formally,

'We welcome you to our village today. The chief will arrive soon to begin the meal. Please be seated.' There were no seats, so we sat cross-legged on wall to wall plaited flooring where long narrow tablecloths overlaid with fresh banana leaves had been spread out. In the company of the men alone, we were to eat an array of national dishes. These were served by the women from a hot stone in-ground oven that had been slowly cooking the food since the evening before. 'Our diet will be new to you, so let me explain,' Akanisi volunteered. 'In that dish you see a favourite root vegetable we call cassava. It's a variety of sweet potato. We don't only eat ripe yellow bananas as you do, but as a starch dish, we cook green bananas and eat them like potatoes. You can sample them today with the main course. The tropical green vegetable over there is rather like spinach and we steam it in coconut cream. The cream is made by simmering soft shredded coconut flesh in water and then pouring it through a strainer. When let stand, this liquid separates and the thick, semi-solid coconut cream rises to the top. We skim it off and use it in cooking.' On hearing of the spinach-like vegetable, Charlie wanted to know if there was a reward for eating it,

'Is there any dessert?' he tactfully asked, his hopes rising.

'O yes. Just wait till you taste our sweet juicy pineapple and red papaya,' smiled our host, 'and to quench your thirst, we have the refreshing translucent juice from young green cocoanuts to drink.'

When the paramount chief arrived we began the meal and, at the end, applauded his speech which Akanisi translated into English for us. When we had finished and left the table, the women came to eat from what remained and, after them, the children. If there was anything left, the domestic animals had their share. I marvelled at the 'gentlemen first' custom but Kalara, a teaching graduate from a local university, assured me,

'This is an old tradition only practised on special occasions. When we eat in our own home, we all sit down together just as you do.' I admit the explanation did mollify me.

'What did you like best in Fiji, boys? I probed as we drove to the airport for our onward flight.

'I think it was diving for the sand dollars that lay on the bottom of the lagoon. The water was so warm and clear,' smiled David.

'So, how many did you collect? I continued. With some pride they laid out several flat white shells the size of Australian twenty and fifty cent pieces on the table to be counted,

'Um, quite a haul,' I nodded, 'and where are we going next, Charlie?' I asked, but he was not forthcoming. Then after a pause he whispered,

'I think Davie knows.' David was almost sure and suggested,

'It's Samoa, or maybe American Samoa, isn't it?

'Western Samoa first and we will cross the dateline. What do you think that will mean boys? asked John.

'It means we will get there yesterday,' laughed Charlie who thought that must mean we were time-travellers. It did mean, though, that when our plane touched down in Apia, we were in good time for Christmas dinner once again! In the Samoan islands, we discovered an ethnic shift from a Melanesian to a Polynesian population. Differences between these two island peoples were evident in appearance, language, dress, music and custom. When it came to eating, our Samoan friends, Aulani and Fetia invited us to join their extended family and to sit down together on the floor once more. This time we gathered around a large woven mat to celebrate the season. This was spread out on the raised floor of an oval fale (house) where posts supported a thatch-roof and there were no walls. The mat was groaning with an overabundance of in-ground oven baked fare and tropical fruits. No one ate a bite, however, until the chief had delivered a long, apologetic speech about the poor quality and meagre quantity of food on offer. Aulani replied in Samoan on our behalf. In his speech he countered the chief's apology saying how wonderful the quantity and quality of the food was, and what a privilege it was for us to eat under his roof (if not within his walls!). Formalities over, we set to doing justice to the meal. The stopover in Apia was short and when Charlie realised we were leaving he confidently declared,

'Now we're going to American Samoa,' and we were on our way once more for a brief touchdown in Pago Pago. This visit was different for we had no contact with national people. Instead, we helped our fellow resident Australian friends Keith, Marion and three-year-old Chris demolish the leftovers from—you've guessed it—Christmas dinner.

Beyond Samoa, the romantic island of Tahiti was ever beckoning. Taking our leave, we boarded another flight, soaring ever upwards into an azure sky where we glided across a boundless sea until we landed smoothly at Faaa airport, Papeete—too late for Christmas dinner. While we waited at the carousel for our baggage, however, we found ourselves surrounded by several giant coconut crabs, big as dinner plates, scuttling noisily round our feet on the vinyl tiles. Beginning with this incongruity, we soon discovered to our delight that French influence on the Polynesian population had indeed created a warm and welcoming hybrid culture. It was not hard to understand the allure of this part of the world for the French like artist Paul Gauguin. While living there he was inspired to paint what are claimed to be the best of his works. We, too, were enthralled with the beauty of Tahiti adorned as it was with hibiscus and bougainvillea blooming in colourful profusion.

'Whose flowers are these?' I naively asked as kilometre on kilometre of roadside sped by bordered by the lovely blossoms.

'Whose?' returned our friend Michel, a little bemused. After thinking for a moment or two he grinned and concluded, 'Oh, I suppose they're everyone's.' It was mango season in this island paradise and John spied the luscious fruit that freely fell from the avenue of trees along the road.

'Look, they're just lying in their hundreds all over the ground and those boys over there are kicking them about like footballs!' he marvelled.

'Those aren't usually eaten,' reflected Michel.

'We prefer to gather bigger, better tasting varieties to use on the table.'

'Oh wow, the fences are growing!' exclaimed an astonished David as he stared out of the car window and pointed incredulously at a line of border posts.

'It's like this,' explained Michel, while the posts are still green, they are set up to mark the boundary of a property. Because life wants to keep on living, and finding themselves in fertile soil with plenty of rain water to drink, the posts sprout new little branches and leaves. Soon they forsake the purpose of their planting and join their kind as living woodland trees once again.

'How good is that,' sighed David and Charlie agreed.

If this island was beautiful on land, the glories of the sea were of equal fascination. Large colourful fish filled the natural aquariums that formed part of the underwater coral landscape.

Turtles floated and small sharks darted within craggy spaces. Stingrays glided smoothly across the shallow water covering the white coral sand that fringed the nearby islands. Michel's sister, Colette, and her husband, Yves, had a villa on the edge of a lagoon. They invited us to lunch with fellow guests and we dined in their spacious sunlit courtyard overlooking the water. A blend of French and Tahitian cuisine made up the midday menu while the company spoke a Tahitian accented French, liberally sprinkled with indigenous words. With our high school French, we fared poorly at understanding the conversation. However, the atmosphere was redolent with goodwill and we felt very much included. Taking leave of our gracious hosts, a radiant sunset bade us farewell as our plane climbed the skies eastward over the Pacific once again and set its course for the west coast of North America.

A crisp frosty December morning greeted us at San Francisco airport where we climbed into a waiting car and drove north through the Napa Valley to our destination.

'O look Dad, gum trees!' cried David spotting the superior specimens of Australian eucalypt that formed an avenue on each side of us. These would prove to be a modest introduction to the towering Douglas-fir and giant redwood forests we were yet to meet but they generated a nostalgic sense of home in this otherwise foreign land. Our route took us through acres of dormant vineyards where thousands of well pruned vines stood in regimental order. There they waited, knee high in winter grass, for the command of spring to awaken them to new life. The area was reminiscent of the rural campus we had recently left behind. Both campuses sat on the edge of sprawling vineyards though the American wineries were more established than the Australian. When we arrived, we found our new Californian campus, though larger, bore some similarity to our former home. Beyond the vineyard proximity common to both and a dedicated building or two for each faculty, both campuses boasted a flying school with a small private airfield and both offered natural woodland surrounds with native animals, birds and reptiles close at hand.

Aside from our fenceless house in Victoria where Charlie had learnt to walk, our new home was the best we had ever had. There were few rooms but they were large, the furnishings supplied were capacious and the synthetic carpets were thick and shaggy. Next to a children's swing set, there was a Golden Delicious apple tree in the middle of the back garden. When autumn came, we were to watch through our dining room window while the Mule deer leapt over our garden fence and stretched up on their hind legs to harvest the ripened fruit. A feature of our front garden was a large spreading oak. It offered an autumn challenge that taught us the meaning of the American season they called 'the fall.' This tree was laden with leaves and had many relatives, for it seemed to be a favourite amongst species and almost everyone in the street had one. Come autumn, all it took was a single nod from the season and those trees would drop their leaves in an instant. We all had fun at first, rustling knee-high through the dry foliage. We threw it into the air in armfuls, jumped over the raked up piles or landed on top of them. Into the bargain autumn brought wind gusts so serious efforts to tidy up and rid ourselves of the loose debris were daily thwarted. After an hour of vigorous raking that resulted in several piles of leaves, along would come a strong blast and carry them onto the next door neighbour's leafless lawn. Not that this was a winning stroke, because the same surge would bring just as many leaves from the neighbour's garden on the other side, and scatter them right back where our original piles had lain. At this rate, the daily grind of leaf raking lasted a very long time, interspersed as it was with apologies exchanged between neighbours.

To a family, we were blessed with wonderful neighbours. They invited us to meals, took us shopping and liberally donated toys, storybooks and equipment to help us settle in. Older children mentored our boys, teaching them to play American street games, build 'forts' in the nearby woods and, in Charlie's case, to ride on the tray of a red steel wagon while bigger boys pulled it along. It was in the street that Charlie befriended Henry who was nine years old and lived in a house diagonally opposite ours. Occasionally, Henry was not around to play games and Charlie learned he was in hospital. Henry was the son of Paul and Greta Kruger who each carried a recessive gene for cystic fibrosis. Charlie understood this meant Henry struggled to breathe sometimes, so the two would find pleasure in Charlie's favourite pastime—lying in the grass and imagining shapes made by passing cloud formations. Then one day there was a great deal of activity at Henry's house and Charlie went over to see why. Soon he returned, feet dragging and shoulders slumped,

'What's wrong Charlie, is Henry sick today?' I enquired. With tears he could no longer restrain, my seven year old replied, 'Henry died today in the hospital. He just couldn't breathe anymore.' It was Charlie's first close encounter with death and, though he did not want it, he saw it as a rough dark patch he must negotiate in the course of living patchwork.

One day a special treat came in the form of an invitation to both boys. It was from our nearest neighbour, sensitive and kind-hearted Mrs Scott who thought they might like to come and view her precious treasure. The treasure was a substantial collection of Indian arrowheads shaped from sparkling black volcanic glass known as obsidian. These were carefully catalogued and ordered in a lidded wooden box. A few days after their visit to her home, a worried and wistful Mrs Scott knocked on our front door,

'I'm afraid one of my arrowheads is missing and I was wondering if the boys might know where it is,' she faltered. Neither Charlie nor David admitted knowing anything about the lost prize and Mrs Scott left empty-handed, looking somewhat unconvinced. Some days later a beautiful obsidian arrowhead appeared amongst David's cherished possessions. This was a small but nasty scrap to add to living patchwork and it gave me an appropriate jolt, Oh horrors! I thought, fully ashamed and embarrassed at the discovery. I lost no time in giving David a stern lecture on the evils of stealing and immediately marched him, arrowhead in hand, next door to visit Mrs Scott. She received us a little coolly at first, but when David declared,

'I'm sorry Mrs Scott that I took your arrowhead,' and held it up to her in the palm of his guilty hand, she smiled warmly and commended him as she slipped the glistening arrowhead into her apron pocket.

'You've done the right thing to bring it back to me, David. That took courage and there won't be another word said about it.' It was David's first and last attempt at purloining a coveted item.

Charlie, on the other hand, took longer to differentiate between what was his and what was someone else's property. There was an attempt at shop-lifting from the local store where brightly coloured sales items had been arranged on tables at his eye level. When I discovered two of these trinkets in the pockets of his jeans, Charlie received the same stern lecture on the evils of stealing that I had given David. I led him through the same process of personally returning the item with an apology. However, a curious little clock sitting within easy reach at the music teacher's house proved too much of a temptation and it also found its way into Charlie's pocket. This made him a repeat offender.

'You know, Charlie, the police put thieves in gaol. Do you want to go to prison for stealing other people's things?' I remonstrated. This seemed to work and, after returning the clock, Charlie gave up pilfering. It seems stealing was in the genes, though, for I had not been above it myself as a child and had caught the ire of my father as a result,

'As a thief, we can't trust you to mix with other children,' he had said. 'You'll have to remain at home on your own while your friends are out playing together and enjoying themselves without you.' The punishment had fixed the problem, though it left an embarrassing piece in my living patchwork I never quite forgot.

Our Californian neighbourhood was careful to share with us some warnings of known dangers in the woods. We were to watch out for the perilous poison oak shrub that could inflict a vicious rash, and to keep our ears alert to the tell-tale castanet of a rattlesnake as it basked on a sunny rock. In this way, the woods promised both pain and pleasure. Nonetheless, pleasure was greater and came from the sound of the acorn woodpecker drilling on the bark of a rotting oak; from the sight of a silvery grey squirrel scampering nimbly up a tree trunk or a young black-tailed deer in statuesque pose hoping to remain undetected.

During our years in California David continued in primary school. The transition from Australia was difficult for him at first as he tried to adjust to a new nonviolent playground. Violence had been the survival strategy for most boys in his school year in Australia and, when under threat, he quickly resorted to it. Appropriate behavioural change was slow in coming to David. This was especially so for the school principal, Mr Bright, who reluctantly helped it along with a caning. There was copious paperwork, endless phone calls and interviews between Mr Bright and me in connection with the caning before it could be administered. Thankfully, once was enough and David got the message.

For Charlie, California provided a chance to sample his first real taste of school. He had already learnt from following David in his first year that an unobtrusive entry and quiet presence brought benefits. As a result, there was no caning for Charlie. Because each pupil practised lessons in his own workbook without reference to a blackboard, Charlie's vision did not prevent him from learning or from keeping up with his peers. When it was time to come home each day, David took about twenty minutes to scramble up the steep hill that led through the woods from the school to our house. Charlie, on the other hand, managed to stretch it out to an hour or more. Lying on his stomach on the trail through the trees, he might watch the slow progress of a small salamander or listen to the song of the red breasted robin. For Charlie, the woods were filled with magic and he was in no hurry to break their spell.

For John, these were days of lecturing in a new teaching environment with different student expectations and different rules. Like David, he too ran the gauntlet of cultural change and was forbidden to wear his Bermuda shorts and knee-socks. These had been the universal fashion in Australia for professionals and businessmen alike and were worn with polished shoes and a short-sleeved business shirt and tie,

'You can't lecture in shorts, John. They're immodest,' announced an elderly colleague. In reality, as shorts go, the Bermuda variety were fairly long, finishing halfway to the knee, so this was hard to understand. Given that no shorts were too short for girls to wear on campus, the rule seemed inconsistent, but John complied despite his doubts.

For me, there was an unexpected opportunity to take up study again. I learned that the spouses of faculty members could take one unit each quarter for academic credit free of charge. I enrolled in a core unit for the B.A. with a major in German. At the same time, I had an interview with the Academic Dean who cleverly cobbled together from past university study, at least half the credits I needed for the degree. What remained were a couple of science units, some history, English and a considerable amount of German. Living on campus as we did, with the two boys attending school, it was possible for me to complete the four year degree in the two years we spent there. All came together to make our two years in California the best yet. Without a doubt, living patchwork in those days was a joyful experience where pieces of brilliant colour blended with bright prospects and unlimited aspirations for the future. I revelled in the good life and consciously forgot it could not stay this way forever.

CHAPTER 11

To Move or not to Move

We had plucked the two summers from our years in California and driven across to Michigan to dedicate them to John's study program. Even then, his ThD required four more quarters of classwork, forty hours of comprehensive examinations and a dissertation destined to take three years. It also meant moving house. After two brilliant years on the west coast, the thought of relocation to the mid-west could not have been less appealing. Though we had accumulated little more than a few additions to our library and a box or two of household effects, a removalist was needed to transport our modest belongings east. In order to prepare the boys for the change, we made it the topic of conversation most evenings.

'We're leaving California and shifting to Michigan soon,' was the essence of the message we tried to convey. Grasping the implications on first mention, David ran quickly to his bedroom and pulled an empty shoe box from the cupboard. In it he put a small tomahawk and a pair of clean pyjamas. His packing done, he declared,

'I'm ready to go.' The information we shared, however, did not seem to register with Charlie who ignored David's preparations and made none of his own. Inevitably, a large truck arrived one afternoon in mid-December and backed slowly into our driveway. John began to supervise the loading of our goods and I was outside watching for the boys to arrive home from school. David was first to emerge from the woods,

'It's the removalist's truck,' I explained. 'They're taking our things to Michigan so we can set up home as soon as we get there.' Unperturbed, he nodded and turned from me to join his dad inside the house. Suddenly, a soulful wail ending in a deep-throated sob arrested my attention. It came from the edge of the woods where Charlie, sighting the vehicle in his driveway, stood stricken. Running up the short stretch of road towards him I called,

'It's all right Charlie, we're all here!' Dashing with equal speed towards me, he hurled himself at my legs and held tight until soothing words finally consoled him. Home would always be highly significant to Charlie and the thought of moving at any time, an unwelcome intrusion into his arena of peaceful familiarity.

As our diminutive Ford Pinto, with its covered roof-rack packed to capacity rolled down the hill and into the Napa Valley for the very last time, I shared in Charlie's grief. My heart cried,

'No!' as tears threatened to escape my eyes.

'Are you sad at leaving, Honey?' probed John.

'Terribly,' I choked and he nodded in agreement. 'It's just that these have been the best two years of our lives and I wonder why they must come to an end,' I lamented. There was no answer so I fell into a silent reverie—could this time ever be equalled for contentment and joy? Would living patchwork be this positive at any other stage in the future? Would so many aspects of life come together again to cast my lot in such pleasant places? I faced the probability they would not, and swallowed hard on the large lump lodged in my throat.

A flat mundane landscape mantled in fresh white snow attended our arrival in Michigan on Christmas Eve. Amongst the uniform blocks of student housing we found the apartment allotted to us for the foreseeable future. Over the next two or three months the snow would fall. It would blow across the lake from Chicago and land in heavy drifts that could reach to the second storey of our building. For those living in a family home, shovelling snow from footpaths and driveways was part of the daily grind, whilst highway agencies spread salt on public roads to lower the freezing temperature of their watery surface. Always ready to make the best of things, children found a playground in the freshly fallen snow. They lay on their backs in its soft whiteness and made 'angels' by dragging their arms upwards and above their heads to create the heavenly impression. They built snowmen and snow caves; formed and threw snowballs and went sledding down the one modest hill in the district.

One particularly cold day, we too decided to go sledding. When we arrived at the hill we found it deserted and an icy wind had begun to blow. Soon, a warmly dressed local approached and spoke through the mouthpiece of a balaclava and several layers of knitted scarf,

'You need to go home,' he warned. 'This weather is too dangerous. There's a wind-chill factor abroad that's lowering the temperature to minus 70 degrees Fahrenheit today. It'll begin to freeze your skin and you'll have irreparable damage from the frostbite. I would advise you to go home without delay.' Whether I was imagining it or not, my face was already tingling and growing numb. In less time than it takes to tell, we sprinted back to the car and hastened to the warmth of our cosy apartment. Chastened by this episode, we were more judicious in days to come in our choice of outdoor activities. We did notice that the flat terrain of the region allowed for cross country skiing and that this was a popular pursuit. Armed with a set of skis and poles apiece, we managed to master the characteristic gliding lope that took us across the surface of the white expanse in a reasonable amount of time. Except for John, who had been on skis from early childhood, learning to ski downhill was a challenge that eluded us until after our return to Australia where we frequented snowfields some years later.

The University attracted international students like us from every inhabited continent of the globe including Australasia. This meant that from the beginning we had a readymade social circle of more than a hundred—all from Australia and New Zealand. We were most fortunate to have been fully sponsored. This rendered us free from financial stress, but not everyone was as well off. Cliff and Joan, with their two small boys Gordon and Mike, had no sponsorship at all. They were dependent on their part-time earnings to keep them in food and clothing, pay rent and school bills, meet university fees and hope no one fell ill or needed hospital care. With these constraints, there was no money for luxuries. One bright spring day, when the snow had melted and the walkways were festooned with beds of tulips and daffodils, I met Joan. I was on my way to the shopping centre and she was returning from it. She had a beautiful voice and was singing quietly to herself when we stopped to chat.

'I'm so happy today,' she proclaimed. 'Listen to what just happened! Our boys have been asking for skateboards for some time. I'm afraid our budget doesn't stretch that far so we haven't been able to buy them. Having two boys means buying two skateboards, of course. They cost $25 each and spending as much as $50 for them is beyond our means right now. The trouble is, every child their age in our housing block has a skateboard and it was hard to say no. I was pondering this with regret this morning when the mail arrived. It included a letter from my mother in Tasmania. Mum lives alone on an old age pension with little cash to spare. Yet, when I opened the envelope I found a note saying she had saved some money and was sending it to us with the hope it might be useful. $25 was enclosed. I took the money and went down to the store right away. I located the skateboards and checked the price. Sure enough, I could buy one for $25 but not two. While I was standing there a young salesman approached me with the standard question, "Can I help you?"

Smiling, I jokingly replied, "Yes, if you can reduce the price to two for $25, you would be helping me a lot."

Looking thoughtful he replied, "Just a minute," and turning away, sprinted to a room at the rear of the store. In a few moments he returned carrying two bright new skateboards—one red and the other green.

"I remembered these," he said. "They're scratched on the underside and we can't sell them for the full price. If you're willing to take two, you can have them both for $25." I was delighted and as you can see, I'm carrying them home with a song in my heart. I'm full of thanksgiving, "Thank you Mum, thank you salesman and thank you God for anticipating our need. You're amazing!" I walked on towards the store while Joan continued home with the skateboards. In her hands she held a bright remnant taken from life to include in living patchwork. I felt uplifted by the story and recognised that entering into Joan's joy added a pleasant patch to my own life and it made living patchwork that much better.

In addition to our social circle from Australasia was the German Club of about twenty five who readily embraced us also. Association with them polished up my conversational language skills no end. Ensconced in the new primary school on campus the boys made friends with fellow Australians first, then Europeans as well as Asians and African Americans. This variety gave them an appreciation for people of a different ethnicity and culture from their own. Consequently, we were severely jolted at the death of the toddler in the apartment opposite ours. His young Kenyan parents arrived on campus shortly after we did, but their baby sickened and died from cerebral malaria within a week of their coming. The entire block was thrown into mourning whilst other African students came to console the suffering pair. We stood at our door and watched the steady stream of visitors come and go. Their tear-stained faces reminded me I was not the only one destined to incorporate dark unwelcome remnants into living patchwork. It really was the lot of all mankind to do so and few would escape the impact of the dull and dismal fragments.

On the brighter side, the apartment next door to ours housed a Korean couple with teenage girls. We could hear them sing like angels through a common wall and watch them float from the building on their way to perform at a concert wearing traditional full length hanbok gowns. Thus attired, they provided a magnificent spectacle fit to arrest the attention of the whole neighbourhood. On one occasion we accepted an invitation to lunch with them and were introduced to edible seaweed as an essential vegetable. This was a first tasting for John and the boys who tolerated the novelty fairly well. Growing up in Northern Ireland as I did, edible seaweed was not new to me. I relished dulse, a variety harvested by hand at low tide from the rocks along the edge of the Irish Sea. So, when offered a second helping I did not hesitate, motioning to my family to make the most of the opportunity too, but they were disinclined to do so. I reasoned that one must have to grow up on such delicacies to really appreciate them.

Two days into the New Year and classes were on for all. Though our ample allowance from Australia was more than adequate, John was invited to teach some classes in the undergraduate school with pay while working on his doctorate. I registered for a Master's degree with a major in pastoral psychology and counselling and added a part-time job as secretary to the Head of the School of Modern Languages. I kept typing both John's and my term papers and theses and was kept at it by the ceaseless drumming of the typewriter in the apartment underneath us. It was occupied by Solange and Pierre, a French couple on a similar mission to our own. We tried to work in tandem with them but they beat us to the finish by two weeks and were gone.

In terms of study breaks, there was a significant six weeks long recess at the end of the summer quarter before the regular academic year began in late September. Because we were spending a total of four summers in the US, we used each of these recesses to make a camping tour of a quarter of the country. When he heard this plan, David, who could happily have made his permanent home in a tent, skipped around the living room yelling,

'Whoopie!' at the prospect. Charlie, on the other hand, already anticipated the long hours of travel with his brother in the back seat of the car and took along his magnetised chess set to relieve the tedium.

For the first two recesses our camping tour took us back to California. During the first of these we journeyed via the northwest from Michigan to British Columbia and dropped south through Washington State, Oregon and into California. During the second, we travelled southwest through Arkansas, Oklahoma,

New Mexico and Arizona before turning north for California. The attractions of national parks, historic sights, Native American lore and theme parks were destined to lure us on. For the latter two recesses we toured the northeast with its history of the founding of the nation, its struggle for independence from English rule and its civil war. Being socially inclined, Charlie wanted to know if he could go to the Boston tea party. That denied, he struck out from our campsite with a fishing rod and headed for one of the small brown lakes of New England hopeful of making a catch. An hour later he reappeared holding his fishing rod upright with its impossibly tangled line that resembled a cloud of candy floss, but with no fish. The episode marked the beginning and the end of Charlie's interest in fishing. Our final recess was spent in the southern states where we met our friends Ziggy and Jane from California. They were in Florida visiting Ziggy's brother Des who had a spacious waterfront home on the Gulf of Mexico. Des was generous spirited and by the time he and his speedboat had dedicated three long days of summer light to us, even I could water-ski with reasonable proficiency. It was Des's repeated assertion,

'You got it made in the shade,' that encouraged us toward success. In driving north from there, we discovered African American history with its cotton plantations and slave trade. This story intrigued and saddened us as we skirted the Mississippi, enduring its oppressive humidity and visiting the mansions and townships of yesteryear. My imagination stirred, I fancied we might catch a glimpse of Tom Sawyer or Huckleberry Finn on the run, but it was only the spirit of Mark Twain that haunted the landscape and hovered over the river.

Recesses spent, we were back on campus for our final school year. More friends from California, Colin and Sue, had come to join us in Michigan. Colin would head up the Department of Religion in the undergraduate school. These two were hospitality personified and I learned the art of rural mid-western homemaking from Sue. She was a daughter of the Pennsylvania Dutch and had all the initiative and industry of her kind. She canned and froze every kind of fruit and vegetable possible as it came into season. Her table was laden with delicious traditional fare for Thanksgiving, Christmas and family birthday celebrations. Best of all, we were always invited to share in the festivities and any loneliness we might have felt was quickly banished by the genuine joy of their company. Commonly, Americans eat with a fork in the dominant hand and use a knife only when necessary. So, when we first met Colin and Sue, it was a source of wonder for them to observe five year old Charlie plying a knife and eating peas off the back of a fork with skilful dexterity,

'Get a load of that little guy with the knife and fork. Ain't seen anything like it!' marvelled Colin.

Working at a fast pace John managed to finish his dissertation ahead of schedule and to successfully defend it. My Masters was also complete and all that remained was graduation. This was cause to celebrate and we did it with a trip to the local Dairy Queen outlet where we ordered a swirling two-toned ice cream apiece to signal our success. Admittedly, this was not the only festivity we enjoyed with numerous friends and associates as well as lecturers, employers and supervisors taking us out to brunch and lunch or inviting us home to dinner.

It was mid-April and more than three months before we were due back in Australia.

'Let's spend the extra time in Germany,' suggested John. 'Maybe we can stay in my folks' spare apartment and I could attend some post doc lectures at Heidelberg University.' Ever keen to brush up my German, I enthusiastically agreed,

'I'd favour that and it'd be a good experience for the boys.'

The week before we left, David's school friend, Albert, came to extend a lunch invitation to us on behalf of his family. They were from Taiwan and both parents, Grace and Kim, were lecturers at the university. We were to come in a few days' time and the menu would be traditional. Once seated round their dining table, we discovered shades of our Fiji experience as the women and children were nowhere to be seen and only Kim and our family were eating. We were served nine courses by Grace who moved between the kitchen and the dining room wearing a white apron and waiting on us course by course. Grace and her mother stayed in the kitchen for the duration of the meal, preparing dishes from quails' eggs to fried rice while the children ate at a small table near them. Apart from Kim, none of the family joined us at any point and, ultimately, he farewelled us at the front door. We did not get a chance to ask, but we suspected we had experienced a special treat and mealtime for them normally, followed the western way. Certainly, we had made many friends in Michigan and were sorry to say goodbye. However, Europe was calling with its historic towns, spring blossoms, May markets and, of course, family. Packing up, we left the US behind but its contribution to our living patchwork would never fade.

We arrived in Frankfurt to discover that thirteen years had made marked changes in our circle of German friends. The church youth group had moved away, married, and one had died. I decided that living patchwork is living with transience as much as anything, and transience does not countenance permanence. Ours is a life of change for all where nothing can stay the same. How glad I was that God offers permanence in the life to come!

As ten and eleven year olds the boys were ready to test the social opportunities on offer out in the street. They spoke no German and the youngsters of the neighbourhood spoke little English. Somehow they managed to communicate and even strike up a friendship or two.

'What I can't understand,' frowned Charlie, 'is why all the girls are called "Martina". Maybe it's the only name they have for girls in Germany.'

'Ah no,' objected David: 'Remember how so many ladies in America were called "Linda"? I reckon it's about being trendy.' And that seemed to settle the matter.

Our last two weeks in Germany were spent with John's brother, Georg and his wife Trudi. They had no children of their own, so they took delight in spoiling David and Charlie. With days full of visits to the funfair, rides on elephants and shopping for new sets of clothes, the boys had the time of their lives. While Georg and John were alike in body type, Georg had known more of 'the good life'. His near-new suits were from Italy and of the finest quality but had become a little tight for comfort. They were, however, a perfect fit on John and found enough room in his suitcase for the rest of our return journey. Destination Australia was our next and final move. Reluctantly we took leave of family once again and boarded the long-haul flight from Frankfurt via Singapore to Sydney and home.

CHAPTER 12

To Pet or not to Pet

'For home to be truly home it needs children and pets,' was commonly said. I soon discovered that both leave indelible footprints on the fabric of living patchwork. Cats had been the preferred household pet in John's family and dogs in mine, but for one reason or another, other animals had found a place in our lives as well. During my childhood, Dad had run an exotic reptile exhibition where I learned to feed green South American iguanas and an African crocodile. Knowing they were not venomous, I was comfortable handling snakes of the boa constrictor kind. So Dad loaded an Australian diamond python onto my shoulders and instructed me carefully,

'This species kills its prey by suffocation. It coils itself around an animal and crushes it. When you handle it, the trick is to keep uncoiling it from the tail end. If you do this, it won't be able to get a grip or apply significant pressure.' Sufficiently cued, I grasped the dry, scaly serpent with both hands and proceeded to uncoil it as it tried to encircle my slender frame. Its long muscular body was very strong, but staying diligent at the task, I managed to avoid being squeezed to death. It was a business venture for Dad, so none of these creatures were esteemed as family pets.

This was especially true of the snakes that, in an effort to stay warm, slept through the day in a hessian sack under the settee in our living room. Being nocturnal, their activity began after we had gone to bed. In the morning we would discover them asleep, innocently coiled atop their sacks. However, the evidence was they had been out and about during the night,

'Look!' cried Mum, 'those vases on the mantelpiece are precariously near the edge, and the books stacked neatly on the occasional table are now askew. Oh, and look at the mirror! It's covered in two-pronged imprints. Those snakes have been roaming around this room and been mesmerised by their own reflection in the glass!' Shocked, we turned to Dad for a response,

'Ah well, I suppose I'd better house them somewhere else,' he sighed. Apart from reptiles, there were tanks of tropical fish in several rooms of our house. Before the advent of television, friends, neighbours and anyone interested would come to watch the colourful fish swim, feed and produce their young.

In truth, Dad was an incurable animal lover who called himself 'a naturalist' but without the scientific credentials to authenticate the claim. To my delight he arrived home one evening with a box pierced with a series of air holes.

'Thought you might like these,' he grinned as I lifted the lid to reveal two blue/grey chinchilla rabbits.

'Oh Daddy, they're beautiful,' I cooed, picking them up one at a time to gently stroke their silky fur. Soon two velvety black rabbits were added and we kept the four in a hutch stowed behind the coal shed in our back garden. It was my job to feed them with their preferred crop of dandelion leaves which grew in profusion all over the district. One morning Dad summoned me from my room and escorted me to the rabbit hutch. To my horror, lying prostrate stretched out on the floor were the lifeless forms of the two chinchillas. Nearby, two obviously unwell Polish blacks sat motionless, unwilling to get up and walk.

'See what happens when you don't feed your pets?' snapped

my father. 'They die from starvation!' Aghast and unable to bear my Dad's displeasure, I fled from the scene, baffled and failing to understand. I had scoured the fields and roadside verges hunting dandelion leaves until they had become hard to find. Then one day, I had spied several large dandelion plants in the otherwise weedless garden of our next door neighbours, the Williamsons. I found I could easily reach these plants by stretching my hand through the fence and plucking their nearest leaves. I knew they were pervasive weeds and did not think the Williamsons would mind my taking them. Having harvested the leaves, I fed them to my eager rabbits. Mum was aware I had not defaulted on feeding my pets and was puzzled by their sudden death. All became painfully clear when, during a conversation with Mrs Williamson, she learned the dandelions had been treated with a highly potent weedkiller. Alas, my four soft, furry pets had been poisoned!! They all perished in a day and lingering over their stiff little forms I experienced my first real brush with death. For a while, I kept hoping they would wake up, hop around again and nestle in my lap as before. Unhappily, they remained quite cold and still as Dad dug a hole beyond the hutch where we silently buried them all. The loss marked my first taste of grief, and I sensed the reality of living patchwork. Life was a journey of the rough and the smooth, the light and the shade, creating a dappled shadowland of happy and sad experiences as long as it would last.

While Dad had owned a hunter horse, each of my parents had a dog in their youth. Dad had an Irish red setter and Mum a spotted Dalmatian. Dad's love for 'Rolph' went without saying, but to Mum, 'Prince' was almost human. He was bathed and groomed weekly with his toenails buffed and polished to perfection. With the boundless energy of a teenager, Mum would ride a hundred miles and more in a day on her thoroughly washed and polished bike with Prince running beside her. When the soles of his paws wore too thin on the tarmacadam road, Mum would pick him up and peddle home with him draped around her neck. Knowing this background, Dad thought it would be safe to bring home two little pups from a Dalmatian litter. The notion was badly conceived for Mum refused to allow the dogs into her pristine garden where every plant was nurtured to a fault. Dad realised there was nothing for it but to keep the dogs at his place of work where he built an enclosure for them. The pups were a great attraction for me and Dad suggested I name them. One was well formed and beautifully marked with even spots. I called him 'Prince' after Mum's pet and thought it natural to name the other 'King', even though he was not quite as regal. King had a slighter frame, was unevenly marked and when he raised his ears, one sat higher than the other. It was a highlight of my life to visit the pups daily and watch them grow. Then one day on arrival, I could find only one pup.

'Where's Prince, Dad?' I queried. Gravely, my father looked at me; his kind eyes clouded with sorrow and slowly responded,

'With his quick intelligence, King found a way out of their enclosure and Prince followed him. King dodged the traffic to cross the road successfully but Prince was not as fast and was hit by a car. I'm afraid he didn't survive.' The tragedy touched Mum and she allowed King to come home. From that day on, however, she did not put a hand on the garden. King was supplied with a grand kennel located where the rabbit hutch had been. He roamed the district and teamed up with a scruffy stray that Dad named 'Rags-the-Mutt'. The two dogs were inseparable, keeping each other warm through the cold winter months. King was officially mine, but Mum fed him so his most enthusiastic welcome was for her. No matter where he was he would respond to her whistle, especially at mealtime. Nevertheless, he would not eat until she had said the magic words,

'There you are now.' Permission granted, he would bolt it down as though he had not seen food for a week. King hated the bath so I did not inflict it on him very often, except when he had rolled in farmyard dung or was so muddy his black spots were indistinguishable from the white of his coat. Farmers complained to the local police,

'That spotted dog frightens the sheep giving them a twirl round the field every day.' More than once he carried a trophy to his kennel in the form of a dead chicken, snatched from someone's fowl yard. Horrified on one occasion, Mum raked together some dry timber and lit a bonfire (a favourite activity of hers). Then she laid the dead chicken on top of the flames in an effort to destroy the evidence. With barely suppressed giggles, I began to sing a 50's favourite, 'Come to the barbecue and sit by my side.' With guilt and chagrin already at play Mum silenced me with an angry command and ordered me inside. Surprisingly, the suggestion to get rid of King was never made for despite his aberrant behaviour, she had actually grown very fond of him. As for the dog himself, his loyalty was without question. He would often lie eight hours at a stretch in the snow beside my parked bicycle. Evidently, he was waiting for the school bus to arrive so he could accompany me home. Leaving Northern Ireland meant leaving King in the care of a dog lover who gave him an indoor home. This had always been his greatest aspiration and, no doubt, he relished it.

Speaking of chickens, John and I fancied fresh eggs from free-range hens fed on grain as part of our regular diet. This led us to buy four young white leghorns on the cusp of laying and to house them in an existing backyard coop. It was David who treated them as pets. When he was eighteen months old he would sit by their pen and 'talk' to them, share his matchbox toys with them and, much to their animated delight, push handfuls of fresh green grass through the wire netting for them. In general, it was only a trip to the zoo that challenged little David's attraction to animals. Unafraid for himself, he assessed the size of a creature and, if it seemed too big for comfort, insisted on pushing John and me away from its enclosure in the interests of keeping us safe. Having kept us well supplied with fresh eggs, our first flock of chickens eventually gave way to a second and then to a batch of speckled bantams. This last batch arrived as day-old chicks and, while still small, were often found nestled in the cupped hands of David and Charlie. Our chickens were doubtless 'working' pets. We fed and cared for them and they supplied us with eggs—a satisfactory exchange.

During the summer we planted a vegetable garden of radish, lettuce, zucchini, cucumber, runner beans, tomatoes and corn. Winter saw us change the crop to cabbage, broccoli, brussel sprouts and cauliflower. This attracted native animals and it was difficult to preserve the winter produce from marauding possums that descended nightly on the tender plants. A more frightening event was the discovery of a venomous red belly black snake that had taken up summer residence in our cucumber patch. The patch was located near the fence separating us from our neighbour's chicken run with its tempting delicacy for any snake—a daily supply of fresh eggs. John noticed agitation amongst the chickens and spied the reptile slithering towards the fence and the coop. Arming himself with a spade and an axe, he ordered the boys and me inside while he dealt the creature a lethal blow. This event sensitised us to the presence of snakes in the garden, so much so that when David saw a scaly body curled up in a woodpile near the back door, he sounded the alarm,

'There's another snake, Dad. It's in the woodpile!' Again John waged war on the creature but he realised too late it was a case of mistaken identity. Sadly, he raked the lifeless form of a harmless blue-tongued lizard out into the open while we all stood round lamenting its death.

It was not until we took up life in the US that our first real pet joined the family. He was a young budgerigar bought as a hatchling and barely able to keep his balance on the perch in his cage. With little imagination we named him 'Bluey' on account of his vivid colour. We had found the cage at a garage sale complete with ladder, bell, swing and mirror. We installed it in the sunny living room of our Michigan flat and each evening we let Bluey out of his cage. It took him a while to gain enough confidence to step onto the proffered finger but, after a week or two, he mastered it. His next step was to transfer deftly from finger to shoulder and thence to head. From here he would take flight, circling the living room a number of times. Finally, he would land on our shiny table top where he skidded about and picked at the leftover lettuce on the edge of the salad bowl. Or, he might perch on the rim of an empty glass with his head bent low to investigate its contents and only his tail on view. In all of his actions, his only vice was an occasional nip of the earlobe hanging above the shoulder where he had perched. For this misdemeanour he was quickly returned to his cage where he sat complaining volubly for the rest of the evening.

On our return to Australia, wildlife pursued us once again. It was springtime and a family of starlings had hatched in the eves overhanging Charlie's room. Mother starling had flown down into the garden and was calling her youngsters to follow. Sadly, in attempting to leave the nest, two of them had fallen down between the house frame and the inner gypsum wall. Mother and fledglings called to each other for two days whilst the young were trapped within the wall. Charlie was anxious for their safety, but unless we cut a hole in the gypsum lining his room to release them, their fate was sealed. The gypsum had been decorated by John in a wallpaper of geometric design. I figured that if I took a sharp knife and cut cleanly round the edge of the square nearest the sound coming from the little birds and removed the piece, the fledglings could be freed. Hearing the plan Charlie enthused,

'That would be great Mum, let's do it!' John was overseas on a work assignment at the time but I thought his skilled hands would have little trouble replacing the piece when he returned, so we set to work. The resulting cavity was large enough for the chicks to escape into Charlie's room. In less time than it takes to tell, they were reunited with their mother. On his return, John did not sympathise with our method of rescuing the young birds and I felt his displeasure at the action I had taken. It took me back to my Dad's displeasure the day the rabbits died. Though I had not been guilty then, I was content to wear the blame for the release of the small starlings now. I knew John would repair the hole I had cut in the gypsum so, after a sigh, a few tut-tuts of disapproval and a shake of his head, he set to making it as good as new.

Next, it was David's turn to be involved with wildlife. First, a plague of mice infested the chicken feed stored in the unused end of the garage. We caught these in traps and David skinned them, stretching out their pelts and pinning them to a wooden board. From this he developed an interest in taxidermy and went combing the creek banks in his canoe in search of potential specimens. Deceased crested pigeons, tawny owls and marsupial rats that had not yet decomposed, came home to be stuffed and mounted. Once, David arrived with a fine rat carcass but there was no time that day, or the next, to deal with it. I knew it would have to be discarded before he could work on it, unless we froze it. Wrapping it carefully in several layers of thick plastic, we consigned it to our large box freezer. The rat lay there for a couple of weeks before David had time to treat it with the necessary chemicals and work at stuffing it. It was at this point that I told John of the rat and its whereabouts.

'What! A dead rat in our freezer, with our food!! David, get it out right away!' David was only too happy to oblige for he could now openly work on his rat. I was satisfied that the rat could be used, John was appeased at its removal from the freezer and Charlie was more than amused at the whole affair. Not everything in our family went this smoothly, but learning to time things well, did seem to help.

In terms of family pets, the dog was a latecomer. She only joined us when the boys were nearing the end of their primary school years. Sheba was a young fully grown black Labrador mixed with Australian kelpie when she became ours. She was as affectionate as the former breed and as protective as the latter. Her strong loyalty kept her close to us on camping trips, bushwalks, cycling tours and rowing expeditions where she followed the road or swam across the river just to be nearby. Her greatest love was riding in the car where, whether invited or not, an open door was an inducement to dash in and settle on the floor. Like an only child, Sheba enjoyed sole pet status in the family until her world was shattered with the arrival of Cassidy and everything changed.

Like many lads of twelve, David was keen to own a horse and living in the country made it possible. Horses were expensive but a friend from down the road had rescued a beautiful tall slender grey gelding from the knackery and brought him home. He had been an obvious show piece with a proud step and elegant gait. However, an accident had severely damaged his right hindquarter and his rear right leg was lame. He was a high horse to mount but with a few riding lessons, alongside daily feeding and watering, David had learnt to manage him well. This was no mean achievement for when I mounted the horse he would spread his front legs apart like a giraffe at a waterhole and refuse to budge an inch no matter how much I commanded him. Cassidy lived in a nearby paddock but our back garden was Sheba's domain. Part of this consisted of an elevated transpiration area where a swathe of lush green grass flourished. I knew this would provide a singular treat for the horse so I called,

'Hey! David! How would you like to go down to the paddock to fetch Cassidy. I'm sure he'd love a spell at grazing on the lawn grass.' In a few minutes David was back astride his horse. Dismounting, he led him gently to the transpiration area where Cassidy began to devour the luxuriant treat. Meanwhile, Sheba discerned an invasion of her territory and suspected divided loyalties on our part. She was not about to share our attention with anyone else, so she crawled on her belly to the very spot where Cassidy grazed. Whining pitifully, she inched nearer and finally rolled on her back to lie directly under the horse's muzzle. Aggression was not in Cassidy's nature so he waited patiently while we removed the jealous dog and allowed him to resume his feasting. Ultimately, the two learned to tolerate each other's presence but only at a distance.

Though Sheba accompanied us, a move to the city meant saying goodbye to Cassidy. Because she liked his name and felt sorry for his poor lame leg, an Irish girl took him away to live on her fertile property and to see out his days dining on lots of lush green grass. Sheba lived with us in suburban Melbourne until age and infirmity took her on her last walk. This was to an adjacent property where she stretched out on the driveway and breathed her last. By this time the boys were university students living away from home. So, John lifted Sheba's remains into a wheelbarrow and covered her with her blanket. We walked slowly into some bushland near our home and there John dug a deep hole and buried her. Emotionally, she had been his dog. Of all the family, he had shown her most affection and it was he who grieved her passing the most. As for grief itself, it was yet to bite us hard—much harder than we could ever imagine.

CHAPTER 13

To Grieve or not to Grieve

Pastoral counselling was a branch of ministry well suited to my personality. It had the added advantage of being less sight dependent than other specialties. Apart from this, I had no idea how my newly acquired skills would be used. I was interested in being a 'people helper' and if others felt I had this ability, I supposed someone might recognise it and employ me.

When we returned to our campus in Australia, the Principal, Doctor Morris approached me,

'I understand you took the opportunity to complete a Masters while you were in the States,' he began. I nodded my assent and he continued. 'We could use your skills. We need someone to teach Family Studies in the undergraduate school and take some lectures on pastoral psychology and counselling for our graduate students. Would you be interested?' Student counselling services were in their infancy at the time so a second invitation came,

'We're a student/faculty association on campus and we'd like someone with your expertise to set up a student counselling service for us. It would involve career advisement, personal problem solving and coaching in people skills. Would you consider it?' Consider it! I was thrilled at the prospect of both offers and readily accepted. Because my top priority was the care of my own family, I restricted my on-campus involvement to work within school hours. This meant that when mid-afternoon came and the boys alighted from the school bus at our front gate, I was standing on the doorstep with a glass of fruit juice and a welcome hug for them. While the day's activities were still fresh in their minds, I listened as they recounted instances significant to them. Of course, they took care not to mention any misdeeds on their part, but sharing a report on general happenings did help to strengthen the bond between us.

This was especially important as they entered the teen years and life became more complex, communication more guarded and activities more peer oriented. Except for the words of Ted, a specialist in child development and a wise friend, this drift towards independence would have troubled me.

'You don't have to worry,' Ted calmly assured. 'Teenage peers are only influential in superficial areas such as the dress modes of the moment, social activities of the day and friendships may be fleeting. Core family values will prevail especially if there is little question as to what these values are. Even young people who reject the faith of their families end up living by much the same set of values as their parents. They just drop the religion. The kids to be pitied are those with no clear consistent family values to internalise in the first place. They tend to rely on their peers to show them how to live. This is often where the trouble starts because their peers have no life experience and little ability to parent.'

I meditated on this for a moment and then teased, 'Is it the parental role to police?'

But he took me seriously, 'Ah no, it's to provide—and not just money. Stable parents represent good choices and they don't deviate from what these are. In other words, they don't confuse their kids by shifting the goal posts in the game of life. This means they provide security on several fronts. It comes from the wisdom they've gained in being a whole generation ahead of their kids. They can share what it means to be secure, to find social success and to prepare sensibly for a future career. One thing parents can't be, however, is friends with their teens. Teens will not accept them acting or dressing like their friends. They don't want their parents to abdicate the role nature has allotted them. They want Mum and Dad to be a reference point for living. Teens and young adults will appreciate this most.'

Soon Ted's words would help me accommodate a painful outcome when, in recognition of his good results at the end of his high school years, we offered David a trip to Europe. It was John who spoke,

'You've done so well son, we'll take a trip to Europe to celebrate. There's much there you haven't seen yet.' David was thoughtful for a moment and then replied,

'I'd really like to go to Europe, but not with you and Mum. I'd prefer to go on my own or just with Charlie.' It was a blow to my sense of family cohesion and I keenly felt rejected but John rallied quickly. He remembered being nineteen and leaving his parents to travel to Australia on the other side of the world, and it was for at least two years, so he replied,

'All right, you can go on a trip to Europe on your own if you wish. You'll need to do it economically and we'll pay.' David took us at our word and managed to tour most of the continent on a shoestring budget. In the process, he visited several countries with their capital cities, major attractions and prominent museums. It is what we would have done anyway, but the thrill and novelty of independence made it much more appealing to him. Reluctantly, I accepted that it must be so.

It was during these years that a transfer back to Melbourne came our way. John took up a new position that meant travelling around the South Pacific and beyond. It involved multi-island itineraries, administrative councils, conferences and short-term intensive schools for the academic upgrading of pastors. At the same time, a large private hospital in the same vicinity as John's headquarters invited me to join their chaplaincy team. I was to visit patients, preach homilies, christen babies, be present at the end of life and officiate at funerals. I would also help run the hospital's counselling service, conduct in-service training sessions on a variety of interpersonal skills for hospital staff and prepare couples with a series of classes in pre-marital education. During the six years that ensued both boys completed high school and were making their way through university—David in medicine and Charlie in economics.

During their yearend breaks they worked to earn some useful cash. For one particular summer, David secured three months full time employment as a wardsman transferring surgical patients to and from theatre and collecting neonatal blood samples from tiny feet. Amongst other things, Charlie found a short-term job with the State Roads Department recording the registration numbers of vehicles as they crossed a major city bridge. It is debatable whether his work was effective, though, for he could not see to read the number plates,

'What do you write down?' I queried, somewhat bewildered.

'I write down what it looks like to me,' he shrugged. Wages earned in commercial cleaning and as labourers on building sites taught them both the value of money. At the same time, their plans to continue training for a place in a profession were validated if a permanent job in the unskilled sector was to be avoided.

Undoubtedly, change means challenge and for Charlie and me there was always the added factor of low vision in the context of change. Even so, living patchwork was manageable, if not easy, as we negotiated the difficulties of our changing worlds reasonably well. After all, had we not been living with our large dark patch for as long as we could remember? Nor were we alone in facing it but were helped by the generous support of John and David who drove us without complaint wherever and whenever we needed transport. If life had nothing more difficult to offer we counted ourselves fortunate. Life is neither predictable nor ordered, but amounts to a collage of crazy patchwork pieces; some large with an all pervasive impact; some small having little effect. Living patchwork always includes the dark with the light, the rough with the smooth, the hard with the soft and the difficult with the easy. This was a truth we were not to forget.

Early spring had arrived in 1991 and it was end of term for the boys. Two months remained till David's graduation and Charlie was nearing the end of his first degree. It was Friday morning, September 6 and I was at work. John had been in Samoa for two weeks of ministerial upgrading and was flying back to Melbourne that afternoon. The next day he would turn fifty-one and the layer cake I had baked to celebrate was still to be filled and decorated when I reached home at 1.00 pm.

I had begun to visit patients on the maternity ward when my pager sounded. The flashing ID alerted me. It was Rob, director of chaplains, summoning me to his office. I pondered the unusual call for it was not like him to pull me off the ward on a busy Friday morning. Making my way to his office, I tried to guess at the reason but nothing could have prepared me for what came next. I was ushered in and the door closed behind me. Several people of prominence stood uneasily around the periphery of the room and Rob's chair was occupied by Dr Bayles, CEO of mission headquarters where John worked. I was offered a seat and Dr Bayles began to speak,

'I deeply regret that I need to share some very bad news with you. There's been an accident and John was involved.' I could see he was trying to break the news gently, but I interrupted,

'Is he dead?' I needed to know but was not prepared for his one word reply,

'Yes.' It did not seem real. It felt like a dream and I would soon be waking up to a normal day. Long before the news touched my emotions my mind was begging for answers so I pressed,

'Where is he? How did it happen? Where was he going? Who was with him? A car accident—who was the driver? Was anyone else killed or just John? Answers were offered but they did not register with me. Numb with shock and rigid with emotional control, I sat upright and immovable in the chair. Tragic news travels fast, however, so one by one and in groups, co-workers came to express their sympathy. Slowly the truth began to filter through the haze of unbelief that had clouded my baffled mind. Then I lowered my head with a sigh and whispered,

'Oh, my poor Darling!' At that point a tall slim figure stepped forward and Peta, the gentle director of nursing, was cradling me in her soothing embrace. Trying to regain my grip on normality I blurted, 'I haven't finished my work for today. I'd better go back on the ward.' At this, Rob spoke up gently,

'Someone else will care for that. You're not on duty anymore today.' The hospital was a kilometre from home and walking both ways was usually part of my daily routine. But that day, a colleague took me by the arm and guided me to his car. We arrived at my house within minutes and, immediately, I called my parents. It had been two years since they had moved from the west coast to live a little north of us. On hearing my tragic news, they tossed a few essentials onto the back seat of their car and were with me in an hour.

Of our boys, Charlie was first to arrive home. My dad met him on the driveway and attempted to prime him with an enigmatic,

'Brace yourself, son.' With that Charlie came inside, more puzzled than prepared by this advice and blanched white as a sheet with shock when I broke the news to him. David was told of the tragedy by Bruce, a friend living nearby, who travelled the forty kilometres south to the hospital where David was in residence to tell him of the heartbreak and bring him home to us.

Thus began several weeks when life was at a standstill. Streams of mourners came to visit—some to support and others to be supported from our meagre store of emotional strength. Arms full of flowers were delivered daily, and though we had no appetite, the fridge and freezer were fully stocked with food by generous donors. Dad took on the job of fielding phone calls while Mum watered and sorted flowers while she wept.

There were three funerals in all. The first took many days and was held in Samoa where funeral practices there meant we had to wait. Finally, John's body arrived in a lead-lined coffin that Australian law forbade us to open. We simply had to trust that his remains were inside. The second was a morning funeral in Sydney. It was led by a retinue of men from Samoa in national dress and was attended by several hundred local friends and supporters. I sat in the front row of the church in my widow's weeds holding Charlie close to me on one side and David on the other. A sixty strong guard of honour lined the aisle as we led the mourners out to the foyer. Here we received them one by one as they shared their condolences with us. The third was a graveside service held in the afternoon in the cemetery near our old alma mater and scores of friends were in attendance. Again we sat in the front row but this time, John's coffin lay at our feet. When I first noticed it, incongruity threatened to lighten my mood with an involuntary smile. John was highly circumspect and thoroughly European in his elegant understated tastes. This was characterized by a sophistication deeply rooted in fine quality clothing and careful colour coordination. As a consequence, the sturdy sealed Polynesian casket draped in a large covering of heavy white lace and decorated with large artificial flowers could only add a touch of irony to the sight. It did serve to distance me emotionally from the scene, for the funeral simply did not fit with John. In fact the Samoan presence was rather overwhelming and it felt like I was attending someone else's affair. A redeeming feature was that men of our choice spoke. They had known John for decades; had worked beside him and their grief was almost as keen as our own. After the service, many friends supplied refreshments and expressed condolences. In the end, despite the kindness, care and compassion, we were drained beyond belief and relieved to climb into the car and make our weary way home.

For days before and after these funerals, I spent most of my time receiving visitors, taking phone calls and answering mail.

This continued for three weeks, and when the flow began to slow, I turned to my stalwart parents, 'Mum and Dad, you've been marvellous. You've kept my home running, tended to all kinds of extra tasks and had to cope with your own grief. It's time you had a well-earned rest. Please feel free to go home and recuperate.' Torn between not wanting to leave me and needing to go, they finally went with a promise to come again soon.

With the boys at study and no heart to return to work myself, I was eventually alone in the empty house. That was when I began to grieve in earnest. Sobs shook my frame and tears blinded my eyes as I wailed in mourning for the one I had lost. For most of the day, I would lie on my back on the settee, de-energised by depression and immobilised by inertia. When night came I had little sleep—just the constant longing for John to come and fill my arms once again. I tried to pray but focus failed me and I understood the wonderful spiritual support there was in the prayers of others for me. Because John's work had usually taken him away for weeks at a time, I kept expecting him to walk in, having returned from the last trip. The sleep that did come was fitful. During it, I would hear his voice calling me; only to wake with a start to the empty space beside me and the silence. The last time we had been together, David had driven John to the airport for the trip to Samoa and I had jumped out of the car to take my leave of him.

'I don't want to go on this trip,' he had confessed as we stood side by side on the footpath, an exceedingly sad expression passing over his face. Good at jollying I countered,

'It's only for two weeks and you'll be back again.' He lingered uncharacteristically on the footpath and watched us drive away until we were out of sight. It was the last time he saw us.

David coped with his grief by burying himself in work but Charlie was immobilized. He visited the university campus but attended no lectures and sat no exams. I was given compassionate leave from the hospital with no expectation to return to work until I felt ready. The boys could well have done with such a provision but there was no leave for them. Two weeks after the funeral we acknowledged David's birthday, but with little celebration. The usual light-hearted joy associated with family events was missing. Instead, we sank into a melancholic malaise. No one wanted to hear or play John's favourite music, often expressed in a minor key. If we were confronted with it unexpectedly, its evocative strains reduced us to tears. This was particularly true of hymns, arias and choruses from certain operas and the movements of several symphonies.

In terms of grief recovery, hardest for me to accomplish was the long term task of forming a new identity. Parts of my life were still intact. I was still mother to my boys; colleague to my work associates; friend to my social circle and child to my parents. I retained my job as chaplain but half of me seemed to be missing. I was no longer the wife of a prominent church leader and would no longer have a place by his side. There would be no more world trips accompanying my husband on work assignments. I would no longer automatically share the esteem and respect accorded him as his wife. In reality, I had been one of two people—now it felt like I was half of one. I was a widow and I recoiled from the designation. Over time, friends and relatives on John's side began to recede as those on my side drew nearer. Some we had known for decades carried their friendship on and remained friends of mine alone. But, I had lost the haven that had told me precisely who I was. I felt myself float away from the secure mooring I had always known, only to be washed up I knew not where. At the deepest level my identity in Christ had not altered for nothing could change that, not even my own death. My struggle was only for this life but it was trial enough. Living patchwork is only for this life too, but it is our present reality and its irregular pattern is our lot.

CHAPTER 14

To Part or not to Part

John's sudden death was not my only misery, nor was it the worst. Living with a collection of rough dark patches that chafe, rub or irritate takes patient endurance on the road to adjustment. The fact there is no guarantee things will change for the better makes acceptance essential, for living patchwork does not always promise recovery. This means unattractive remnants that do not yield to improvement can become permanent additions to the pattern of life.

A born optimist, I had always lived by the dream that best efforts bring best results and, because of parenting practices that were grounded in love, ours was destined to be a happy, cohesive family. My belief was that external circumstances may buffet us from time to time, but our internal strength would prevail. There was no mystery to this for the source of our internal strength was faith in God. Nonetheless, for some years before John's death a spiritual turbulence began to trouble our otherwise tranquil home. This became more evident as arguments and objections to faith increased. Perturbed, I had eventually raised my fears with John,

'Our answers seem powerless to convince anymore. I just don't understand what's happening in our home.' It was my first close encounter with unbelief and I did not know how to relate to it. John, on the other hand, had once raised his own questions and, finding unbelief unappealing, had chosen faith. He offered me an explanation,

'Our son knows he has a choice. If he chooses unbelief, he can discount biblical authority and enjoy the freedom he seeks.'

'If he does that, wouldn't he have a bad conscience? After all, we've emphasised that truth is to be found in Scripture.'

'There is a way he could live comfortably without believing. It is to adopt a moral relativism where decisions about right and wrong would be at his own discretion rather than from an external source. A person's conscience can accommodate very well to this approach and it results in little pain.'

'But what would he do about sin, salvation, and eternal life? Wouldn't he want to inherit the eternal life promised by Jesus?'

'You're talking about biblical concepts. I don't think our boy believes there is a heaven to inherit, so why strive for it?'

'Is unbelief so appealing that a person would forego all that God offers just to hang on to it?'

'It's very appealing. It makes a man his own master completely. He knows no God and, as a consequence, forfeits all the benefits promised to those who do. Of course, belief is more than mental assent, it means commitment to follow.'

This conversation was hard to hold because I did not want my son to forego anything good. It left me very uncertain, not knowing what the future might bring. I was grateful, though, that while John lived we all kept attending church, and I kept hoping and praying our son would reconsider. With John, daily worship at home and weekly attendance at church had been the habit of our lives. Now that John was no longer with us and I had become 'head of the house', I needed to gauge the spiritual climate prevailing under my roof. This led me to stand one evening in the middle of our living room floor, dwarfed by the height of my two tall sons, and pose the basic question to them,'

'How do you think we arrive at truth—is it with our own intellect or do we need guidance from God?' Obviously, they had already considered this for the response was without hesitation,

'With our own intellect,' offered David.

'With our intellect, but under God,' added Charlie.

'Then who has the ultimate authority over what I accept as truth?' I pressed.

'I do,' David affirmed.

'God does,' countered Charlie. It was the beginning of a parting of spiritual ways and I believed from that point on, these differences would serve to fracture the fundamental unity we had always known.

Psychology had taught me that moral weakness and relational imperfection are often concealed by defence mechanisms. On the one hand, these serve to make us appear and feel innocent of wrongdoing in our own eyes. On the other, they may help to deaden the pain of an unwanted reality. Denial is one of the most common of the defences available to us and I readily resorted to it. Sometimes I was able to block from my mind the implications of my son's unbelief. In this way, I could pretend all was well and avoid the need to deal with the emotional impact. At other times cruel reality broke through and my grief became greater and more profound than any I had yet encountered. I knew that where there was belief, other losses, even death, were only temporary because the believer would live again. As a family of believers, I had only ever considered this possibility for us all, but what was I to do with the certainty of eternal loss because of unbelief? I could not bear the thought! In moments of extreme despair I contemplated bargaining with God to let me change places with David. My hope was for him to be sure of eternal life, even if I no longer had that option. Horrified by the consequences of my own thinking, I shrank from the notion with a shiver. It was not that I did not want to make the sacrifice; I just could not imagine the superficiality and cold emptiness of life without God here and now. This is what my choice would imply and there would be no escape from it. Having known the unspeakable joy of walking in the light of God's love with the profound peace and comfort that comes from knowing him, the bleak alternative of a Godless existence had no appeal for me whatsoever. The upshot was, I strengthened my relationship with God and drew ever closer to him.

There was a price for me to pay, however. For years after the parting of our spiritual ways, I struggled with guilt and self-blame. I felt there must have been some unrecognised weakness in my parenting that had led to this result. My heart ached and I cried in desperation,

'Where have I gone wrong?' I found an answer in realising I was not the only parent to face this situation. Others had teenage children and youth who, for one reason or another, had chosen to live without reference to God. All of these suffered and lived in the hope that the parable of the prodigal son would be replayed in their family. For some it was. There were people like Gerry and Sue who told me all four of their teenagers had left God at the end of high school in search of freedom in a bigger world,

'Naturally, they also left the church and I recall how torn apart and desolate we felt,' remembered Sue. Then Gerry brightened,

'After a few years they came back to God and to church. I asked them why they had returned, 'It's because there's nothing out there, Dad,' was their candid comment. I guess my kids realised that, but not all do.' I was glad for them but Gerry's final words cut me to the quick. I was painfully aware I had one who had not returned and was showing no signs of doing so. Because of its significance, this kind of grief engulfed me like a funeral pall and I was powerless to shed it. Sometimes I could be objective, telling myself I had done everything humanly possible to lead my children to choose eternal life. What my son did with my efforts was his choice. This was cold comfort, though, and I found myself resorting to sadness and gloom when I was confronted by painful reminders of what could have been. Finally, I decided that love can hurt quite badly and it would be good if I could just not care.

The trouble was, not caring was out of the question. Not only did I have a mother's love that defied indifference, I also knew the core of the Christian ethic was about caring. Indeed a care that stretched beyond mother-love, past family and friends and even to enemies was basic to Christ's teaching. Because of their connection with Christ, believers could expect to experience and express a quality of love that was second to none and far exceeded any of the natural loves known to man. I was no stranger to this love. It was my own motivation and God-given empowerment for all my relationships. I could not curb its flow, and especially not to my son. Thus I was caught by my own worldview. In terms of living patchwork, this was the darkest and heaviest of all my ugly unwanted pieces, fragments and scraps sewn together.

Of course, there were some beautiful patchwork pieces too. At the end of high school before they enrolled at university, John and I had offered both boys a year at language school in Europe. Although David preferred to postpone his gap year until after medical school, the offer was taken up immediately by Charlie who spent half the academic year in France and the other half in Austria. While in France, he joined a choir that toured Spain and Portugal during the summer break. As part of their itinerary, the group visited a cathedral and assembled to sing under its central dome. As happens, their voices were amplified and enriched by the contours of the space they occupied and the splendour of the resonating sound captivated Charlie. It was then that the years of exposure to Christianity and a firm belief in the Bible culminated in an encounter with God and Charlie committed his life to Christ.

Several weeks after that fateful Friday when the news of John's sudden death was delivered to me, I discovered another rich piece to add to living patchwork. Because of my own loss, when I returned to chaplaincy my ministry to the grieving took on a new authenticity and people could recognise I was talking from personal experience. I found I could be of much greater help to those facing death, whether their own or that of someone close, and this new reality led them to readily accept my words.

Having become a single individual once again, I discovered I was forging a new social identity that was mine alone and no longer ours. Things had changed and people related differently to me. Some drew nearer sensing my need of inclusion and practical help. Others drew back, unsure of how to communicate in light of my recent loss. I connected more closely with female friends as we worked out in the gym, went for a therapeutic massage, ate together in cafés or just walked and talked. On the whole, men treated me with less reserve, if not less respect, and I was readily welcomed into mixed company. It was clear I had begun the transition to a new identity but what would it be like? The challenge was daunting. Having all but lost my close connection to John's world, I foresaw I would lose touch with his family, his work colleagues and with some of our former friends. In a sense I had to create a new self and the task seemed unnerving and protracted. Whether I wanted the transition or not life would bring new people, new experiences and new values to light, changing who I was. At forty-nine my identity was not going to undergo a radical reconstruction but a significant renovation where the new would blend with some of the old and replace what was gone.

Over the next six months I began to emerge gradually from the torpor of grief to take on a more active social life. Good friends drew ever closer and I was included in new ventures with new associates. For a while I continued to receive more visitors than usual. Some of these had also lost a partner. Like me, they represented long-term marriages and their personal experience in dealing with their loss made their visits relevant. Occasionally one would make a dire prediction, 'You never get over it completely you know' or, mournfully recall, 'Nothing is ever the same again.' These comments were discouraging, but when grief survivors talked of their recovery, of new interests and changed direction, I could identify and was helped.

One such survivor was Leo, the husband of my friend Marie. We had been next door neighbours five years before and Marie and I had formed a warm friendship. Highly hospitable and a great cook, Marie had invited us to their home for dinner more than once. One such occasion was to welcome Leo home from a trip to China. This was our first meeting with him and we found him to be a gentle, retiring man with a twinkle in his eye and a ready dry wit. A medical doctor by profession, Leo was head of a busy general practice and when opportunity arose, harboured a love for overseas travel. During the intervening years a mutual respect had developed between John and Leo with an appreciation for one another's professional expertise.

Normally, Marie was not fond of overseas travel but Hawaii did attract her. Leo was delighted with her enthusiasm at the prospect of a trip to Polynesia. They departed Melbourne with a plan to explore the region thoroughly by visiting several of the islands in the group. But, the trip was destined to end in disaster, for before it could finish, Marie had fallen seriously ill on Maui, the second largest island of the Hawaiian group. Accommodated in a holiday condo, Leo had called for an ambulance, but by the time it reached them, Marie had already passed away. Leo, traumatised by her sudden death, returned to Australia devastated. Almost a year later on Polynesian Savai'i, the second largest island of the Samoan group, John was killed in a car accident and, shocked beyond belief, I was devastated.

Because of the similarity in our circumstances and the nature of our two losses, Leo and I had much in common. Gradually, the purpose of his visits moved from support because of past pain to an interest in the present and a focus on the two of us. I had seen what a loyal and caring husband he had been to Marie and was confident we could have a successful relationship too, so I encouraged his attentions. We began to see each other often, and although we felt a little foolish at the notion, we finally confessed to our five adult children that we were 'dating'. While we each loved our own children dearly, we had positive connections with one another's family as well. In light of this, it was natural for us to seek and to value their opinion on our association. We were relieved to learn they respected us equally and approved of our relationship. Four of our children were married themselves while the fifth was living independently. Nonetheless, a marriage between Leo and me would mean a union of two families.

The question was; would we be able to negotiate the differences between us? For me, the discovery of differences was not new. I was aware that while neighbours might share national, regional or even class culture, they also live within the confines of their own individual cultures. This is a sphere filled with the comfortably familiar, and known only to those who share the same living space. While the differences in family cultures impact on values, tastes, behaviours and modes of expression, I knew the key to managing any dissimilarity was clear communication. Also, for Leo and me to successfully join our two lives, each variance would need to be understood and accepted without criticism. Tolerance would be as essential in the process as is oil to the workings of a machine.

Clearly wedding bells were in the air but not for Leo and me alone. Charlie and Ilona, who met at high school, had found in each other the partner of their choice and were due to arrive at the altar shortly before we did. The fact made me smile. On the one hand, I was honoured by the invitation to conduct their marriage ceremony. On the other, I was amused at the incongruity in the order of events. Here I was, getting married after my son and not before him. It gave me a strange feeling. For weeks our days were filled with wonderful wedding plans. Mother and I took a trip to Las Vegas to visit her sisters and there we bought outfits for both weddings. Pink organza and cream lace with pairs of satin and corded silk shoes filled my suitcase on the journey home. Living patchwork was busy accepting fine textures and beautiful shades to be eagerly incorporated into my life. Charlie and his bride were radiant with joy as they exchanged vows before me in the presence of God. Five weeks later, David escorted me down the aisle of the hospital chapel where, surrounded by a bevy of roses and baby's breath, Leo and I were married, once again.

The blended family can have a rough passage to find its new equilibrium, but ours was as smooth as it gets. No doubt this was helped by our not living under the same roof as our children in any permanent way. Everyone's desire to be pleasant and accommodating to the wishes of everyone else was a positive factor. It was also true that our homes were far enough apart to make 'popping in' for a chat quite impractical. Though the raft of differences normally existing between any two people was also present with Leo and me, none of them adversely affected our relationship. Ultimately we could say we had done the best thing possible by deciding to marry each other.

It would take six more years for David to qualify as a neurosurgeon and set up his consultancy in regional Australia. His marriage to Elaine would produce three grandchildren to cheer me and add delightful dimensions to living patchwork. All in all, the grandchildren of our blended family would total seven, and none of mine would inherit the visual limitation common to Charlie and me. In years to come, I would watch them visit us; each sitting confidently behind the steering wheel of a car. This would make me acutely aware of my own inability to do the same and remind me of the last day I ever tried it. Though they took it for granted, their visual advantage was plain to Charlie and me in every way. Without voicing the fact, we were both immensely relieved that this was so and very glad for their sakes.

CHAPTER 15

To Serve or not to Serve

After family, the next most important dimension to life was my job. Chaplaincy had been highly fulfilling and I had no desire for a career change. It had proved to be a niche area where the roles of men and women in ministry were much the same, and equality with my male colleagues was a given. The title 'chaplain' was a leveler. It ensured we were held in equal esteem by most, regardless of our gender. Things may well have remained that way had it not been for a visit from Judy, member of a search committee from mission headquarters. She had been sent to assess my interest in a brand new role, 'The women of our churches need representation and mentoring,' she began. We're looking for a suitable woman with the right qualifications to lead in developing a ministry for them. We think you'd do an admirable job. Would you be interested?' The enquiry was unexpected and I was unprepared for it. It was true I had already been the featured speaker at weekend women's events in several states but was that the essence of this new ministry? How would it fit with chaplaincy at the hospital? Was I about to be asked to leave one post in favour of the other?

The answer to these questions came in a letter of formal request,

'We invite you to the volunteer position of Coordinator for the Office of Women's Ministries.' In a word, this would mean adding a second undefined responsibility with dubious parameters to my existing workload, but with no extra pay. Before refusing, I wanted to know what job description mission administration had in mind; how they saw me fulfilling it and what accommodation would be made for my chaplaincy work. The interview with Dr Bayles left much to be desired. To my question,

'What does the job entail?' he replied,

'Well, you're doing it already aren't you?' After an awkward pause he added, 'It might be advisable for you to make contact with your counterpart in Washington DC and find out from her.' Being single again, I had opportunity to do more than just make contact. With a round-the-world trip already planned with Mother nine months after John's death, I simply asked for an extra return flight from New York to Washington DC to be funded by mission headquarters. They obliged and I was on my way. I had yet to make a final decision about the post, but as I contemplated the possibility of the change, I began to realise how sheltered I had been. By dint of birth and circumstance of upbringing, I felt myself free from some of the social limitation usually imposed on women of my generation. Because this sense of freedom was not felt by women at large, strong winds of change had begun to blow across the societal landscape affecting gender roles. This meant that significant numbers of women were seeking both involvement and visibility in positions traditionally held by men. Over the foregoing twenty years, I had seen opportunity and education fit women for a new independence where reliance on the name and means of a father or husband was no longer a necessity. Women were fast staking out their own identity and marriage had become an option for them—a part of life, but no longer its whole, whilst motherhood had become a choice.

In this climate, Christian women were looking at the anachronisms of the church and wanting change there too. They saw that it was culture, not biblical principle, that governed gender attitudes and behaviours and they were contesting the conventional norms. On our long-haul flight to the States, I confided in Mum, who paved the way with her forthright question,

'Do you think you'll take on this new job? My reply was cautious,

'I must admit I'm a bit reticent. If, in this climate of change for women, I were to take on the post I would find myself pulled in different directions. There would be the radical reformers with strident voices who wanted me to join them; the lobbyists who wanted to write my speeches for me and the good-hearted followers looking for ways to serve formerly denied them. The fact that they're all seeking credible leaders from amongst their own gender does influence me in favour of taking it on, but I'm still to make a final decision.'

I alighted from the New York flight for a pre-arranged meeting at the Washington airport with my counterpart, Rhonda. Because I was unable to see faces in any detail, recognising a person was ever a problem for me and locating Rhonda was going to be a challenge. I did have an idea of her appearance from a photograph but Rhonda had not met me before and had a different woman in mind as she stood at the gate waiting. Needless to say, it took us both several minutes while we worked on a process of elimination before settling on each other as the one to find. Laughing at the awkwardness of our meeting, we left the arrivals area together and made for the VIP lounge. Then, seated in comfortable armchairs, we began to talk in earnest.

'My brief,' explained Rhonda, 'is to foster a ministry for women throughout the world while yours, I understand, is to do likewise throughout the South Pacific region. My committee and I will draw up the general direction for this ministry and develop some useful resources, while you address issues specific to your region and call on us for assistance.' By the time we had spent a couple of hours together, I was getting the impression this initiative for women was more about empowerment than anything else. It appeared to me to be designed to meet the challenges raised by feminism. Rather than adding anything new to the mission of the church, it represented an overlay of women's involvement where only men had functioned in the past. It could be summarised as,

'Move over guys and make room for us. We're here to work alongside you in roles formerly occupied by you alone.' I could see this would imply a paradigm shift that would need diplomacy and tact if it were to succeed.

'An important aspect of this ministry,' continued Rhonda, 'is to cultivate confidence and encourage women in their faith.'

'To this degree it truly is a ministry,' I agreed. Nonetheless, I thought, making room for women in unfamiliar roles, especially those invested with authority, would take a good deal of gentle strength in negotiating with men.

Even though my relationship with Leo was still new, it was a significant factor as I thought about the future. I needed to know how he felt about the extra job and its impact on my time. When I raised the matter, his response was generous,

'I'll support you in whatever you choose to do.' With this assurance, I decided to accept the added load. This was in the belief I could balance it with chaplaincy and maintain a manageable lifestyle. To my satisfaction, things went very well at first. Mission headquarters lay just across the road from the hospital. So, any lull in the demand for my services there allowed me an hour or two to spend on aspects of the ministry for women. There was a problem though, for the two spheres were quite incompatible. I found it difficult to change gears from offering emotional support and spiritual care in the medical world to generating creative ideas in think tank sessions in the other world. At the same time, several weekends of the year were committed to women's events involving me in the real world.

Whether it was due to overconfidence or to inexperience I am not sure, but eventually, I found myself carrying a load of guilt. I was overcommitted to the volunteer job with its lack of parameters while robbing my paid position of enough time. This situation grew increasingly worse over the next two years. Overstretched, I was about to resign from the volunteer job. I came to this decision with a struggle because I thoroughly enjoyed this ministry and could see results for my efforts. Before I could take the step, however, Dr Bayles approached me once again,

'We recognise you're doing an outstanding job. We'd like to invite you to serve in the ministry for women full time. Of course, it would mean you'd be a fully paid member of staff.'

'And my hospital job?' I queried.

'You'll probably need to relinquish that in favour of what we're asking you to do here,' he smiled.

What they were asking me to do entailed extensive international travel. It would include Europe, South Africa and the United States with a particular focus on the nations of the South Pacific. These island countries stretched for thousands of miles from Western Australia east to Pitcairn Island and from

Kiribati south to New Zealand. As I contemplated this, anticipation built inside me and I thrilled at the thought of contact with thousands of women of different cultures, languages and lifestyles who belonged to these nations. Undoubtedly there would be unknown challenges ahead but a sense of certainty was growing within me and I turned to Dr Bayles with my answer:

'Yes, I'll do it,' I affirmed. I knew this acceptance meant saying goodbye to work in a place I had come to call my own. No longer would I walk corridors to visit wards, meet new patients and greet known staff whose faces were as familiar as family. There would be sadness at leaving for ten years is long enough to make a space where one knows and is known. Chaplaincy had given me a window on the world of human emotional need, a sense of the pain of suffering people and an awareness of the complexities of tangled lives. Amidst calls of, 'Do you really have to leave?' and 'We'll miss you!' I stepped out of the hospital to greet a much larger world where the tasks familiar to my daily routine would be multiplied. They would also be tempered by healthier, happier circumstances. Although the job was undeniably big, it was one job with one description and implied accountability to one administration. I was glad to forego the balancing act I had tried to maintain for the past three years and to reach towards a new horizon.

Surprisingly, my new employer did not seem to notice, or if he did, did not comment on my visual limitations. I pondered what it would mean to try to function in a leadership role with executive responsibilities when I could see so little and read even less. I concluded that if he did not make an issue of it, neither would I. Instead, I would find ways around the problem as I always had. Fortunately for me, most travel was by air and a courier service transported me to and from the airport. Pick-up at the other end of a flight was locally organised with plans to deliver me safely to my accommodation. This process also worked in reverse for the homeward journey until I was safely dropped off at my own front door. For appointments closer to home, I would normally be expected to drive, but Leo's support was highly practical and he drove me wherever I needed to go. These commitments were always over a weekend so they did not impinge on his medical practice. I admit, I will be eternally grateful for the kindness of all the significant men in my life. From my father to John, and from David to Leo everyone drove me anywhere with a willing generosity. None of them made me feel a nuisance, nor did they show any reluctance to oblige. Far from small mercies, I count this amongst the big blessings of my life.

Though countless did, not every man I came across added to my blessings. Amongst my many supporters were the few detractors. Sometimes their actions could not have been timed to do more harm. On one occasion the gathering was large with several hundred of both genders in attendance. I was about to mount the podium to speak when an ill-conceived comment came to rest quietly in my ear,

'Why don't you sit down and be quiet as Paul told you to do? You have no business standing in the pulpit. It's not for women.' On another occasion, in consequence of the faint smudge of pale pink on my lips, the censure came,

'You're wearing lipstick in the pulpit—shame on you! You'd no right to go up there in the first place.' In some communities, the appearance of a female preacher was simply too much, and several voted with their feet, vacating the premises as soon as I rose to speak. In fact, the entire group of men at one gathering left en bloc before I uttered a word. Even though my ministry was principally for my own gender, women themselves demonstrated a mixed reaction to it.

'Do we really need this?' was voiced by some. It seemed the change was most difficult for those who opposed the ministry of other women, refusing to support them if they tried to serve in roles previously occupied by men. Some women could not see themselves in public life and wanted to deny that function to every other woman regardless of her ability.

At the same time, a palpable sense of relief emerged from amongst those who recognised their potential and wanted to reach it. Their enthusiasm resulted in diverse kinds of service and they were often motivated to develop creative new ministries not yet tried. On another level, numbers of young women were inspired to train for a career in professional ministry believing the doors of the church were opening for them to fulfil their calling. Women with obvious leadership strengths found they could now function as elders, overseers and mentors in local congregations.

These instances taught me that culture, not Scripture, is the strongest determinant of human behaviour in the churches. I saw that waging war against culture was futile for its practices would be strongly defended by those bound by it. I recognised that people of both genders were most comfortable with the known and if culture was anything, it was a collection of the familiar. However, all was not lost because, over time, the new becomes familiar and culture adjusts to meet the change. I had to believe in this to have hope for the women who wanted to realise their ministry dreams.

The woman who had ministry dreams of becoming a pastor faced the greatest challenge. While a woman was content to work as a volunteer for her local congregation she met with more acceptance than the one who wanted to be a professional pastor paid to function in many congregations. Once again, it was the notion of pastoral authority that threatened most. The earliest female graduates from degrees in pastoral ministry were diverted in their quest for a post as a pastor with a church of their own to shepherd. Instead, they found themselves teaching Scripture in high school, playing house mother to the residents of a girls' dormitory or functioning as a chaplain in an aged care facility. While these were all worthy occupations, none of them challenged anyone's notion of being in charge.

Slowly and over time the wheels of change began to turn. The first few female graduates to be given pastoral ministry positions found it to be hard going. They were chosen in the first place because of their outstanding qualities. Once they took up their positions, however, their authority was immediately challenged; their working methods criticised and their ministry style questioned. This was no job for the fainthearted and several stepped out of the line of fire by returning to more sheltered careers like nursing or school teaching.

By the time we had reached this point, I was due to retire from the workforce. At the same time, a progressive group of Christian businessmen saw the need to support the female pastor who was struggling against cultural prejudice in order to do her work. Their attention was drawn to me as a suitable candidate to provide that support:

'You have the experience and the connection with these women and they respect you. We'll pay you a wage and give you an operating budget to support them.' Experience had taught me to consider my answer and to negotiate terms.

'Well,' I said, 'I do have a heart for the welfare of female pastors, no question. However, I want to retire in the full sense of the word. I don't need extra money so I will work as a volunteer. An operating budget will suffice and I will determine how many hours I'll give to this ministry. Oh, one other thing; I'll do all the contacting by phone and email but, much as it would be ideal, I'll not be travelling around the continent to visit these women in situ. On the other hand, I'm happy to organise special events for them from time to time, so they can get together for mutual encouragement and to learn from more experienced female pastors. This would be on the understanding that you provide me with a special budget for the expenses incurred.' In truth, the group was very glad to find someone who might cause their hopes to materialise so they readily agreed to the terms. For the next twelve years I held hands, lifted chins, encouraged hearts and inspired women willing to battle the odds and remain in ministry. By the end of this period, more women were finding greater acceptance as mainstream church pastors. Prejudice was breaking down to the degree that younger recruits wondered what the older set was talking about when they referred to the struggles of the past.

'They don't realise how hard won the victory has been to ensure they have a place in pastoral ministry. They're taking the past for granted,' was the indulgent opinion of the seasoned. The reality was things had changed so much that the younger recruits were unaware of the battles of the past and could comfortably take for granted much of the ground gained. This is generally so when the next generation stands on the shoulders of the former to reach their aspirations.

If I thought my lot in life meant living patchwork with its varied qualities, textures and shades was difficult, I found I was not alone. There were travelling companions to join me on the ministry journey. Some were courageous women whose lives were affected by good but unpopular choices and who met with rough dark patches as a consequence. Others were fearful women who took the soft option and avoided difficult choices. This also had its consequences. Just as crazy patchwork is strewn with smooth light pieces amongst the heavier scraps, so life continues to make a random pattern, not entirely based on choice but greatly influenced by it. It is the pattern of living patchwork that tells the story of our lives.

CHAPTER 16

To Tell or not to Tell

While living patchwork tells the story of our lives, it is no secret that storytelling has a dubious reputation. Stories are prone to embellishment, distortion and exaggeration to the point where a listener is unable to tell the difference between fiction and fact. Though the telling art is subject to these foibles, a person seeking guidance knows their story must be true if professional help is to benefit them. Aware of this, I had listened to hundreds of stories—each unique, worth the telling and deserving of my full attention. Though the characters varied and the circumstances differed, some of the stories came to a common end. This was surprising and quite unexpected.

One of these was the story of Bernadette. She was born in Ireland, the child of a young single girl who died when Bernie was very small. The child never knew who her father was, but came to live with an aunt in England who took her in from a sense of duty. As Bernie told it, it was a loveless adoption to say the least.

'The girls of the family, my cousins, were older than I, so I always wore their outgrown clothes. Nothing I owned was bought, or made just for me. I remember wearing a pair of old wellington boots, without socks all year round because I had no shoes. I was often told I must show gratitude for my aunt's great kindness in giving me a home, but I always felt I was on probation and likely to be sent away with nowhere to go. I tried to be on my best behaviour—forever striving to win my aunt's approval. I did everything in my power to please her but I didn't always succeed. When angry with me, she'd lock me in the cupboard underneath the stairs and deprive me of my next meal. Mine was quite a miserable childhood but I believed I deserved nothing better. It was only as an adult I could look back and perceive the neglect and the abuse. This was in contrast to the privileges showered on my cousins. It was a sort of Cinderella scenario, I suppose.'

'And was there a Prince Charming?' I ventured.

'O yes, there surely was, but not until many years later. I met Patrick in London while I was in training to be a nurse and we fell in love. It was just wonderful to feel loved by someone and I adored him in return. In time, we married and had three healthy children, who continue to flourish as they grow,' she beamed.

'So, why have you come to see me?' I enquired. Bernie paused for a moment before continuing cautiously,

'I wouldn't want you to think ill of Pat. He's a wonderful man and a good husband and father. It's my fault really. I'm afraid I'm changing—becoming a new woman and it's making things very difficult for him. Naturally, it's putting a strain on our marriage.' In the past it seems Pat had always found Bernie compliant, acquiescent and eager to please. Being so amenable had proved a sure way to retain his love, but she was beginning to see this came at a cost. 'Pat's angry all the time. He was always so caring and considerate, but now he pushes me away physically and swears at me. I can't tell you how much that hurts. It seems the price for a happy marriage is to live under Pat's control. But, at thirty seven I'm growing up at last. I've developed some personal opinions, wishes and tastes that must remain unexpressed or there's tension and conflict. The question is: how do I become the woman I want to be and still maintain a happy marriage? I've come here to ask if this is even possible.'

Pat was resistant to joining Bernie for our counselling sessions so we focused on building personal confidence in her with the hope that she would develop some resilience. She could see that her old strategies of living to please in order to win love and acceptance were damaging and unproductive. At first, she found standing up to Pat with his threats of deprivation and desertion very hard to do,

'I was horrified to realise that living with Pat had the hallmarks of living with my aunt. I thought I'd left that behind when I moved to London.' Refusing to believe any longer that she deserved this treatment, Bernie began to take tentative steps towards independent thought and action. Seeing her determination to carry through with change, Pat began to develop a higher level of respect for her and ultimately agreed to join her in marriage counselling. It was not easy. The road to adjustment was long and arduous requiring Bernie to stand her ground at each small advance until Pat agreed to another aspect of his 'new woman.' At the same time, Bernie often repeated her commitment to Pat to love and care for him. She needed my support in the process of change but it was the added strength that came from her new-found trust in God that really held her up. 'I've tried to assure Pat that our marriage will be better than ever because my care for him will spring from choice rather than compulsion. Indeed, I find these new freedoms rather heady,' she confessed, but her inner change was evident. It was seen in her choice of an up-to-date wardrobe, a short modern hairstyle and a part-time job. One day she visited my office, grinning in triumph. 'Guess what. I've come to register for the new course in pastoral care. It'll take me a couple of years to complete, but I've decided to become a chaplain too!'

Brenda's was another story that tumbled out in the privacy of my office. She was seven months pregnant and her baby would be born in our maternity wing. The first time we met I broke the ice,
'Looking forward to becoming a Mum?'
'Yes, indeed,' she enthused. 'This little fellow will soon be here and I'm truly excited. It's just that I wish the circumstances could be different.'
'Circumstances?' I prompted. Looking down to gather her thoughts for a moment, she continued with slow deliberation.
'Greg and I had been together for eleven years and married for six of them. All that time we spent our weekends and holidays camping, skiing, hiking and travelling overseas. It was a great life with lots of freedom and few responsibilities. Every now and then Greg would say, 'Life's great. All that's lacking is a family. Don't you think it's time we had a baby?' I'd laugh and reply, 'O yes…sometime…but not yet. It wouldn't go well with our lifestyle. Besides, we're both working full-time in good jobs. How would we cope with a drop in income if I stopped working to look after a child?' As my biological clock continued to tick, however, I did think about it more seriously. Then, one day, I heard its alarm shrill in my ear,
"You're thirty three. Don't leave it too long!" In response I devised a plan, but in hindsight it wasn't a good one. You see, I thought to surprise Greg with a pregnancy. I planned to break the news to him when we were three months underway at around the time of his thirty-fifth birthday. '
Great gift,' I silently cooed in self-congratulation. 'He'll love it—can't wait to see his face when I tell him!' It was easy

enough to get pregnant, and though the first trimester was a trial with morning sickness, I hid the fact. It was a relief when I saw that Greg suspected nothing. At last his birthday arrived and I woke up early alert with anticipation. Stretching out beneath the covers I looked over at Greg, fast asleep on his pillow,

'Wow, have I got a birthday present and a half for you,' I whispered lightly stroking his dark hair. Then, careful not to disturb him, I slipped out of bed to dress and prepare his favourite breakfast. I abandoned all thoughts of my usual morning walk for I wanted to linger in the unhurried moment and to savour his response when I shared our wonderful news. We sat on opposite sides of the table to eat as I silently rehearsed the speech I'd prepared. Then, rising to my feet I stood before him, ominously patting my abdomen and declared,

'Happy Birthday, Darling. Here's my birthday gift. You are now a father-to-be!' While I'd had three months to get used to the notion of motherhood, this was a shock announcement for Greg. The colour drained from his upturned face and he looked totally stunned for some seconds. Finally, he found words and stammered flatly,

'Oh, that's er...wonderful news.' I'd expected him to spring from his chair, grab me around the waist and spin me dizzy with delight. He didn't do this or any of the things you read about in romance novels. In the awkward silence I heard myself apologise for having sprung the news on him and for having acted independently with my decision.'

At this point Brenda paused and took a deep breath. Clearly, there was more and it was going to be hard to tell.

'We were six months into the pregnancy when we came home from work one evening. After dinner we sat together in the living room as usual, each cradling a nightcap to warm our hands.

It was that quiet, cozy time of day when people relax and intimate conversation is easy and unhurried. The mood was odd, however, for Greg was unusually agitated and anxious as he began to speak, 'We have to talk,' he blurted and his manner was urgent. "I need to tell you that you're not the only woman in my life, Brenda. I have a girlfriend as well—name's Sonya. The truth is you are six months pregnant and so is Sonya. I can't put off making a decision any longer. The question is; do I go with her or stay with you? It's taken me a long time to decide but I've made up my mind; I'm going with her.' Too stunned for words, I watched him leave the room and the house. With his bags already packed, he took no time to hop into his car and drive away into the silence of the night.'

I sat for a moment trying to digest Brenda's story. Then I whispered,

'So you were left to go it alone.'

'Yes I was, and I don't mind telling you my fury was white hot. I wanted to kill him! Ultimately, however, the experience did bring me closer to God. I'd never been particularly religious, but I could see that people who were had the kind of strength I needed to face this.' I saw Brenda several times before her confinement and visited her when little Jordan was born. All the while she had been grieving the loss of a happy future, the loss of her husband's support and her baby's loss of a father, not to mention her changed financial circumstances. As part of the help she needed, she had found a divorce recovery group in a local church. The other members of the group were struggling with similar issues and she found great support in meeting with them. Eventually, when Jordan was a year old, she joined the church's Bible study group and took a course in pastoral care,

'I'm now a sort of chaplain,' she smiled. 'I'm there for those who are hurting because of life's hard knocks. I'm trying to show them that God cares too because that's what I've learnt and it certainly helps.'

Yvette, Shirley and Emma were amongst the many seeking solace in my office. Each had serious marriage problems compounded by catastrophe. For Yvette it was a freak accident that happened on a school .camp. Her eldest son Jason, a fifteen year old, was running downhill through the bush when he jumped and landed on top of a large flat stone. The impact dislodged the stone and as he ran, it came crashing after him. Catching up with him, it pinned him to the ground and crushed his chest claiming his teenage life. For years after, Yvette struggled with the loss. It had been the blow to finally shatter her fragile marriage. Bereft of her son and stripped of her husband's love she lacked purpose and motivation for living. She tried to mend through a series of self-talk strategies and a healthy balanced lifestyle. These helped to a degree, but when she reached the end of her resources she came deflated and fatigued to utter an admission,

'Recovery seems impossible for me. There's something fundamentally amiss in what I'm doing. I've read that I should look in the mirror and find some inner strength by telling my reflection I'm a worthwhile person. Trouble is, the reflection is of me—the disintegrated woman I've become. Grief and depression have robbed me of any sense of personal worth. How can I base a better future on a broken self?' Clearly, Yvette needed a dependable source of emotional energy that would help her build belief in a better future.

'I don't believe you'll find personal worth by looking to yourself either,' I agreed. 'Actually, no one finds worth in looking to themselves. Healthy self-worth depends on the approval of someone else. It's good to know that the one who created us in the first place, I mean God, is also an unfailing source of approval. It's extra good if his approval is humanly endorsed by the affirmation of parents, a husband, or even our children as they grow. Should our human sources fail, however, we still have the unfailing approval of God to form the foundation of our self-worth. After all, he's the one who knows us even better than we know ourselves.' This was a new concept for Yvette but she grasped hold of it. Slowly it helped her come to terms with the devastating tragedies filling her life until she eventually found a new way. Years later, while I was visiting a friend in hospital a hand touched my arm and I turned to see Yvette's smiling face. 'Look, I'm wearing a chaplain's ID,' she grinned. 'After what I gained from you, I decided it was time I gave something back. So I took the chaplaincy training course right here in the hospital. I've been working on the wards for three years now and loving it.'

When Shirley came to tell her story she felt trapped in her marriage. Her husband, Ian, was twenty years older and did not enjoy good health. Their five children were grown and gone from home. In self-absorption Ian had emotionally withdrawn from Shirley leaving her lonely and isolated. Struggling with poor communication and very little affection, she needed a safe place to talk and be heard without criticism or judgment and my office provided the place. Normally punctual, Shirley arrived for her appointment one morning uncharacteristically late. She was out of breath, ashen faced and trembling with shock.

'I'm sorry I'm late but Chrissie's in trouble,' she panted. Her youngest daughter had always proved a challenge and now there was a new crisis. Shirley assessed Chrissie as having no ambition, little direction and less self-discipline. She had refused the offers her well-to-do parents had made to support her while she attended university or trained for a career. Rather, she had chosen to live on government unemployment benefit in preference to getting a job. 'She left home recently and went to live up-country in a commune but came home this morning saying she'd been raped. Ian is shattered but won't talk about it. I'm afraid she might be pregnant or have picked up an STI, or both. I've made an appointment for a medical check; if she's willing to come, that is. She's twenty-one and can refuse, of course.' To Shirley's relief there was no pregnancy, but there was a genital herpes infection. Over the years since that event, Chrissie never did find a firm pathway through life, never worked for a living and never married. Ian passed away some months after the alleged rape and in late retirement, Shirley was still supporting Chrissie who lived with her permanently. As for Shirley, she did summon the strength to accommodate to the problems admirably,

'Oh, I'm managing on a liberal supply of God's love. He's the one I've found to be reliable,' she smiled ruefully. Long after my years of working in the hospital, I found Shirley one day at the entrance to the chapel. 'I came to join you,' she grinned. 'I completed the course in chaplaincy and am working on the wards. Best thing I could have done. I've also discovered why you chose to be a career chaplain—it's just so rewarding to bring comfort and blessing to people when they need it most.'

The story of Emma and Phillip began well. The two sat in my office glowing like a pair of teens caught up in a brand new romance.

'We want to get married,' said Phil and Em agreed.

'We'll be like the Brady Bunch,' he enthused. 'I'll be

bringing three children and Em two, to make up our new family.' In truth, both had come from an earlier divorce and, in the interim, Em had had two relationships. The youngest of their children was Phil's son Simon. He was eighteen and Em's two sons, Justin and Steve, in their early twenties, were living independently. Phil's divorce was more recent than Em's, while he and his three children still lived in the house that had always been their family home. The new dimension was that Em would move in with them.

'I've never known a man as wonderful as Phil. In fact, this relationship is too good to be true,' sighed Em. For years after the wedding they seemed to live happily together until one day Em sank into a deep depression,

'I'd love to talk,' she confided. 'Can we meet somewhere?' I chose a small restaurant with poolside tables and padded chairs. Here we settled with a virgin piña colada and an hour at our disposal. Em began, 'I've been in a very dark place. At first I was delighted to join Phil and his children in their house. I believed that together the five of us could make a healthy, happy family. There was much I needed to learn, however, about how families like ours might function. It turned out Phil's children were at the centre of his life. His first commitment was to them. That put me in second place, an outsider really, with no clear position and no real place in the family. I felt like a tagalong with no voting rights—an add-on of little consequence. Admittedly, I was jealous but Phil seemed unconscious of the problem and just kept living for his kids.

It wasn't long before I felt I'd lost him emotionally. He was fully invested in them with what I considered 'over-the-top' support in terms of time, attention, emotion and money. They were young adults, capable of supporting themselves, but Phil kept giving them considerable sums of money, our money, in loans that have never been repaid. Over the years, he gave them hundreds of thousands of dollars. When it came to our retirement, we could only afford to move into a small two bedroom unit in a retirement village. We gave nothing to my sons. After all, they weren't Phil's children were they? I know I'm sounding cynical but I nearly didn't stay with him. It was only the total commitment we'd made to each other that kept me in the marriage.'

'I take it you are still in the marriage?' I observed.

'Eventually, I recognised the emotional void in my life and knew I needed to find my own happiness. So, I took on a volunteer reception post at the hospital. This forced me to look to the needs of others and to stop feeling sorry for myself. Needless to say, it went a long way towards lifting my mood. I was enjoying my work and had been doing it for twenty years when Coral, the head of volunteers, phoned me out of the blue,

'Em, you're just the kind of person who'd make a great ward chaplain,' she said. 'You've got warmth, empathy, and you care a lot about people. Why don't you take the training on offer and give it a try?' You know, I never thought I'd be suitable for chaplaincy—too far beyond my abilities, I believed. But I took Coral at her word and made enquiries about the course. The rest is history for I've been a volunteer ward chaplain ever since. For whatever use I might be in the role, I've found my niche and it has helped me put our family issues into perspective. I have a much loved interest of my own and it defuses some of the old pressures. Things are better between Phil and me too. His three children are middle-aged now and it helps that they've settled permanently in Western Australia near their mother. Thankfully, we're on our own at last! The good news is my depression has lifted and life seems worth living once again.

Whether recognised or not, it seems living patchwork is the story of everyone's life. Blocks of vibrant colour, parts in a pastel shade, scraps of shadowy grey and remnants of gloomy black are pieced together to form the pattern of our daily lives. Sometimes we go about collecting the fragments and sometimes they're simply delivered to us. Our task is to take them up and integrate them into the whole that we may make of life a beautiful, useful and worthwhile thing for our own enrichment and for the benefit of other people.

CHAPTER 17

To Hear or not to Hear

Stories with a good outcome are always a joy to hear even if they do not reflect reality in the life of everyone. On the other hand, stories with a sad ending are generally hard to hear for they cast a gloomy shadow over the course of life. When an unhappy outcome is part of our own story, we naturally look for healing from the emotional pain it has caused. The trouble is the process of recovery may be long and uncertain while the conclusion is yet to be reached.

It was a Wednesday morning when the phone rang and I heard nurse Kerrie's voice.

'We have a sad situation here in Maternity. A couple, both medical specialists have lost their baby and we need a chaplain.' I entered the private hospital room to find a slender, sensitive Laura propped up on a cloud of pastel pillows, her husband Gerald at her side. In the maternity wing, babies generally stayed in their mother's room for much of the day but there was no baby here.

'This is so hard for you and I'm truly sorry for your loss,' I began. Then Gerald spoke.

'Because the Maternity staff has been wonderful, we'd like to say 'goodbye' to our little one here in this caring place.' Through her tears, Laura agreed

'We want to remember her life, such as it was, and secure

her a place in our family. We don't want her to be forgotten.' I nodded as Gerald continued.

'Would you be willing to conduct a memorial service for us in the hospital chapel and help us say farewell?'

'It would be a privilege,' I quietly assured, 'and shall we name her at the same time?

'O yes please, that would be so good,' nodded the grieving Laura. I didn't know if we could. We had wanted to call her Madelaine, but…'

'Then Madelaine it will be.' I smiled, and after praying with them, left to set about making the arrangements.

Gerald ordered a rosewood cot to be set up at the front of the chapel. The Maternity staff tenderly clothed the little stillborn in a dress and bonnet trimmed with delicate ribbon and lace. They slipped her discoloured hands into a pair of miniature mittens and put tiny bootees on her deformed feet. When she was ready, they laid her gently on a soft white sheet and covered her with an embroidered quilt. The top of the quilt was carefully arranged to shield her small disfigured face from curious eyes, while fresh spring flowers adorned the chapel and clustered softly around the pretty cot. Several family members arrived and sat at a respectful distance while the bereaved parents came in last and took their place beside the polished crib.

Gerald's arm was about his wife but Laura's eyes were fixed on the tiny form. In place of tears, she wore the adoring smile of an entranced mother who gazes for the first time on the face of her newborn child. Nor did she lose her focus during the time the service was in progress. Soft music played as the memorial drew to an end and the family filed out of the chapel to wait in the foyer. Still, Gerald and Laura lingered inside the quiet space, unwilling to leave little Madelaine's side. They needed time alone with her to sorrow, to weep and to comfort one another.

When they emerged from the chapel I went with them to the exit door where they turned towards me. Firmly clasping my hands in theirs, they bid me goodbye and I watched as they walked away to face the full impact of their loss. Now it was time to confront my own emotions with their need to disengage from the scene. A sigh, some tears, a few words of self-talk,

'Oh, the privilege and the pain of the chaplain!' would help me regain control as I walked towards the hospital wards to meet the rest of the day. I knew that to truly share in the sorrow of another takes its emotional toll. On the other hand, the dismal parts of life are never quite as bleak for the one who supports, as they are for the one who owns them. It is they who must embrace them and allow them to become a part of living patchwork.

After hours 'on call' duty was an essential part of the chaplain's role. It meant attending to whatever emotional and spiritual needs arose on any one of the ten floors in the building. From orthopedics to cardiac care and from kids to cancer the sole chaplain on call responded to all. It was early evening and I was on call when my pager sounded. The call was from the cancer ward and the Nursing Unit Manager was on the line,

'Lucy, in room 12, is asking for a chaplain, can you come up?' I arrived on the ward to discover Lucy had advanced breast cancer with secondary tumours in other organs of her body. She was forty-seven—my age, and had two children in their early twenties—just as I did. Her husband was a professional who dressed in a suit and tie and frequently travelled overseas on work assignments, just as mine did. In appearance, Lucy was tall, slim, blue eyed and blonde haired just like me. Even in personality we were similar, but with one difference; she was dying and had unfinished issues on her mind. With so much in common, it was easy to fall into conversation with Lucy but she led me away from what we shared to what she alone was facing—her fear of death. Firstly, she needed to talk about the past,

'I've done things I'm not proud of,' she began. 'I've had a drinking problem and some other things that have put me in the bad books.' I wondered whose 'bad books' so I asked.

'Oh, I just don't know what to do with all the guilt,' she sighed.

'There is an answer for that,' I whispered. 'Just hand it over to God; he's in the business of removing guilt.'

'You mean even mine? she questioned incredulously. 'I've been pretty terrible, you know.' I did not know, and did not need to know.

'He specialises in forgiving people who've been pretty terrible but you don't have to take my word for it. There are plenty of stories in the Bible where he simply forgave and that was it. In fact, sometimes he didn't even wait to be asked. People who were burdened with their past mistakes walked away free and full of joy because of his forgiveness. Would you like to hear one of the stories?' I offered. Lucy's reply was eager,

'Oh yes please, I'd love to hear it,' and like an expectant child, she slide down under the bedcovers and focused on my face, so I began,

'One day Jesus was teaching a crowd that had gathered to hear him. Suddenly, there was a commotion as a group of religious men, dragging a naked woman hurried towards him with bitter accusation on their lips,

'This woman was caught in the act of adultery. The law of Moses says to stone her. What do you say?' they demanded. Now the common teachers of the day would have agreed with the men. Yes, stone her, they would have urged, but not Jesus.' At this point in the story Lucy's eyes lit up and she sat up a little, clasping her hands around her knees.

'What did he say?' she wanted to know and I continued,

'In answer, He presented them with a problem.

'All right,' he said. 'Whoever here is without sin, let him throw the first stone.' Agitated, they looked around from one to the other in dismay. They all knew of their own shortcomings and probably knew some of each other's sins as well. One by one they began to slip away, leaving Jesus alone with the woman standing in front of the crowd. The irony of the story is that Jesus was the only one there who was without sin, but he didn't throw a single stone. Instead, he asked the woman,

'Where are your accusers, didn't even one of them condemn you?'

'No Lord,' she answered. Then he uttered the sublime words that everyone wants to hear,

'Neither do I condemn you. Go and sin no more." At that Lucy's eyes grew moist as she drew in a deep breath and tentatively asked,

'Could that forgiveness be for me too?'

'Indeed it is. That's the whole point of the story. You see, anyone who wants it has that same forgiveness and it's free.' Over the next few weeks Lucy grew weaker but each time I entered her room, she smiled at me with a radiant joy for she had peace at last. The last time I saw her, her family was there and it was clear she was saying 'goodbye' to them. Two young adults stood nearby. They were Lucy's children and her daughter, Michelle spoke to me.

'You know, Mum has found such peace here. Would you please pray for her?' I nodded and we formed a semi-circle close to Lucy's bed. There we thanked God for her life and committed her future into his hands. We were relieved to know that because of her faith, even though she might die, a bright new beginning was guaranteed.

Whether old or young, problems are for everyone it seems. Those of the young may seem transient, even trivial to an older generation that feels it has lived long enough to have faced 'real' challenges. I might have been tempted to agree until I met Kate, a student nurse, who walked into my office one Thursday morning. There was good reason for Kate's visit. She was the eldest of four siblings and had been at odds with her mother for several years. Conflict had escalated to the point where Kate had been turned out of the house at sixteen.

'While I felt lost and forsaken by my mother, I was lucky to find lodgings in a school-friend's home. Access to my own family, however, continued to be denied me.'

'What about your father?' I queried.

'Oh, Dad didn't agree with what Mum had done. He was most uncomfortable with her disowning me. Actually, he saved the day for me because he supported me by meeting my expenses so I could finish the last two years of high school.' While her father's support was good, it was not enough to heal Kate's hurt. Coupled with an inherited tendency to emotional fragility, the damage caused by years of maternal hostility and final abandonment had ensured Kate would suffer from bouts of debilitating depression. 'Sometimes I feel so low it takes all the strength I have to just get out of bed,' was her frank admission.

At twenty-one and love-starved, Kate came seeking a source of positive regard and genuine affection from an older woman. She was a highly intelligent girl with keen personal insight, so she knew where the root of her problems lay. Though she reminded me occasionally of the useful things I had said, I doubt it was words that helped very much. What seemed to matter more was the consistent acceptance she felt. We would end each session with a hug and I suspect that was a major part of her reason for coming. I did not mind, for I sensed it was what she needed most. Beyond those years, further training qualified Kate in cardiac care and she became the manager of a large unit.

In the meantime she met and married Mel, a mild-mannered man fourteen years her senior. Having children was important to Kate but, sadly, it did not happen easily. After several disappointing attempts at IVF and a dangerous pregnancy, at forty-one she finally brought little Amelia into the world. Amelia was to be Kate's only child and, disappointing though this was, it did free her to deal with the heavy emotional burdens still to come. These were imposed in part by her dysfunctional family who seemed to reel from one crisis to another while from a sense of duty, Kate carried their problems. Amongst these was the drug addiction of a younger brother, the emotional lability of a sister, the catastrophic financial decisions of a brother-in-law and the divorce of her parents.

Struggling to find solutions for everyone else left Kate exhausted. Though Mel was a caring father to Amelia, he found it hard to hold down a job. So the burden of providing for the three of them fell squarely on Kate. As well as this, Mel's lack of initiative left Kate fully responsible for caring for the home completely. It meant she was often physically spent as well as emotionally drained. Amidst all this, Amelia was growing up.

'Having her was the best decision we could have made,' reflected Kate. 'She brings such joy into our lives. She's always been happy and helpful, not to mention academically strong and the spiritual leader of her peer group at school. Really, I don't know how we came by her, but I'm so glad we're her parents.'

Her words prompted my response.

'God is a generous giver. I guess he could see you needed a particular blessing to help you cope with trials. Maybe that's why he sent Amelia.' Amelia was not the total solution to Kate's problems but her presence did lighten the emotional load and make it a bit easier to carry. Prayer helped too, though it needed to be revisited often to keep Kate's demons at bay. Talking to God was important but when her emotional resources dwindled to the point of depression she needed some human support as well. Resisting antidepressants as a long-term solution, a workable strategy with a healthy lifestyle, timely support and trust in God emerged for Kate. Despite some ups and downs, this kept her functioning well and it is how she made the best of living patchwork.

Patches of a different shape came to our office manager Corrie. She was a bright bundle of pleasant efficiency and functioned as the organisational hub that kept our chaplains' department running well. Soon after she had married Mike, it became obvious a pregnancy was beyond their reach. Nonetheless, in their view, it was children who made a family complete so they decided to adopt a boy they named Geoff and a girl they called Kym.

'We were so fortunate to get the two of them. They've been the delight of our lives. They're both in high school now, you know. Soon they'll be all grown up.' As we chatted one day It was clear that Corrie had received news of the Australian Adoption Information Act of 1990 but it did not perturb her.

'Our kids are diffident about meeting their birth parents. They say,

"You and Dad are the only parents we know or want. If our birth parents were prepared to give us away, we're not sure we want to know them."

That was until the day a well-presented middle-aged Roberta walked into my office and confided,

'I had a baby outside of marriage eighteen years ago. It was taken from me and I never saw it. I say 'it' because I don't know whether I had a boy or a girl but I've never forgotten. Now we have this new adoption information law I'm keen to find the baby I brought into the world. The agency that organised the adoption no longer exists I'm told, so I came to ask if you'd be willing to help me locate my child.' The irony was that subsequent to the birth of her baby, Roberta had married Frank, the birth father and together they had produced three more children—all boys. Meanwhile, Corrie and I had spent five years in the same department which gave us opportunity to chat about our children once in a while. As a result, I learned some of the details of Kym's adoption and when Roberta arrived with her story, I grew suspicious that there was a connection.

My first task was to try to contact Petra, the woman assisting in the small adoption agency involved. Though long retired, in harmony with the new law, she released the names of the two families and my suspicions were confirmed. Roberta and Frank were the birth parents of Kym while Corrie and Mike had adopted her. Roberta's first need was to know the gender of her baby and then to try and arrange a meeting. My excitement mounted as I contacted Roberta and asked her to see me.

'I have some news for you,' I began

'You know something about my baby,' she guessed. 'Have you found my child?'

'Yes, I believe I have,' I assured her and recollecting her urgency to know the child's gender, I gently asked,

'What is it you most want to know about your baby?'

Soulfully she looked up at me and said,

'Did I have a boy or a girl?'

'You had a little girl and she has grown up to be a beautiful young woman,' was my reply. Roberta sat for a while confounded, trying to take in the information. At last she confessed,

'I always wondered, but after three boys, I didn't dare hope she'd been a girl. Do you know her name?' Of course I knew it. Had she not called at the office a number of times to see Corrie?

'I think it'll be easy for you to find out more and perhaps to arrange a meeting,' I suggested as I handed her a card with Petra's contact details. Roberta left my office glowing with happy anticipation. She was on a mission and could at last fulfil it. As I locked my office door to leave for the day, Corrie was tidying the front desk oblivious to the interview I had just had with her daughter's birth mother. Walking away from the building, I determined to let due process take its course.

A few days later I arrived at work to find Corrie a little tense.

'You'll never guess what. We've been contacted by Kym's birth parents. They actually married each other and now they want to meet Kym.' I feigned surprise, 'Oh and how do you feel about that?'

'Well, now we have this new Adoption Information Act, I guess they have every right to make contact. So does Kym of course, though she's not that eager. I think curiosity will get the better of her though, and she'll probably agree to a meeting.' When a meeting did take place, Corrie was quick to report,

'Kym met her birth family last weekend.'

'How did it go?' I ventured. 'Well, she was intrigued to discover that, as well as a set of birth parents, she has three brothers who are biologically related to her. I was naturally anxious, but I must admit it helped when she confided,

"They're nice people but I couldn't call them Mum and Dad—that's who you are. I feel comfortable calling them Aunt and Uncle and the boys can be cousins. I'll be happy to visit them, but I have one brother and that's Geoff. We've grown up together and we're family."' Corrie was obviously relieved. Whatever she might have feared, there was no threat to her and Mike's relationship with Kym. She was still their daughter and was happy to remain so. Kym was also happy to have some answers to her questions of origin and to find some missing pieces to complete her personal identity. To that degree she was grateful to her birth parents for initiating contact and for letting her know who it was that brought her into the world.

Inasmuch as self-knowledge provides a foundation for personal identity, this was a crucial discovery for Kym. The Adoption Information Act did not always facilitate the kind of communication that brought the best results, but like everything else, it was a part of living patchwork for those impacted by it and called upon to make yet another life adjustment.

CHAPTER 18

To Work or not to Work

Whether birth children or adopted, some people are a standout regardless of their origins. That was my assessment of Monica. Wherever there was a need, be it for a hot meal, some company, a listening ear, a lift to the railway station or an hour's childminding Monica would be there. She seemed to have a sense for knowing just when to offer help and what kind was most useful. This had led to the community styling her their 'angel of mercy'. On one occasion, while Leo and I were lunch guests at Roy and Monica's table, she began to tell a fascinating story. As we listened I heard her quote,

'It isn't everyday a beautiful blonde walks into your office and tells you she's your daughter.' Beautiful was an apt description for Monica was gorgeous. Standing about 172 cm tall and perfectly proportioned she had a crown of loose golden waves cascading down her back. At the same time, wide cheek bones, a finely chiselled nose, full feminine lips and expressive eyes defined her lovely face, while the whole of her frame was wrapped in a flawless golden skin.

'I always knew my sister Jane and I were adopted and came from different backgrounds,' she confessed. 'Our adoptive parents, Pete and Olive, were quite open about our origins. They truly were the most wonderful parents to us. They gave us every advantage possible and I love them dearly. However, I always had a longing to know who my birth parents were. So, when the Australian Adoption Information Act made it possible to find out, I went on a search to discover them.' Astounded at her courage, I asked,

'And were you successful? I mean, did you actually locate them?' Inwardly the thought struck me, 'Would it not be better not to know in case of disappointment? You could visualise them just as you want them to be, without taking that risk.' But Monica responded,

'Oh yes I found them and with very surprising results! Firstly, I located my birth mother, Patsy, and found she was part Aboriginal. She told me she had had a one-night-stand with an army officer and I was the result. When she discovered she was pregnant she got word to my birth father and he sent her £100—enough to pay for an abortion at the time. That was the end of his involvement but Patsy didn't terminate my life. Instead, she carried me full-term and when I was born, she put me up for adoption.'

'Having found her, did you stay in contact with each other?' I probed.

'Yes, to some degree but we're not close. Patsy lives at a considerable distance from me in a different state. Besides, Roy and I have two girls and as far as they're concerned, Pete and Olive are their grandparents.'

'What about your birth father? Did you find him also?' Monica thought for a moment before replying,

'As with most adopted children, locating my birth mother was my primary need, but she gave me sufficient information about my birth father to begin a search for him as well. I'll admit I was curious to know what kind of man he was. I discovered he was the CEO of a large company in the city where I lived so, one day, I phoned his secretary and made an appointment to see him. When I arrived he was in a meeting with someone else. While I waited, the door to his office opened allowing the visitor to leave. Just then I caught a glimpse of the CEO sitting in a chair with his back towards me. At that moment, a shiver coursed through me like a shockwave for there, folded on the desk in front of him, were my hands!' By this time my attention was riveted on Monica and I leaned forward to learn what came next.

'Soon I was ushered into his office and invited to sit down. I didn't want to give him too much of a jolt. After all, he didn't even know of my existence. So I began cautiously.

"Hello Mr Bradfield, I'm Monica Dewar and I've come to meet you because I believe I might be related to you."

"Well hello," he smiled. "Related you think; in what way?" At this I began to piece together a picture of the little I knew of his time in the armed forces over thirty years before and of his contact with my birth mother. I reminded him of her pregnancy and told him of her unwillingness to terminate it.

"In fact," I concluded: "I'm the child who survived—your child. You see, I'm your daughter." Somewhat stunned, Charles Bradfield leaned back in his large leather chair and scrutinised me carefully. At length he spoke,

"I certainly can't deny what you've told me. One look at you tells me you're mine. I must admit, it isn't every day a beautiful blonde walks into your office and tells you she's your daughter! Please tell me more. Are you married? Do you have children?"

"O yes, I'm married to Roy. He's an architect and we have two small daughters in primary school—Emma and Abi. We're a privileged and happy family," I hastened to assure him, though I struggled to understand why I felt I needed to do so. In my view, the meeting with Charles was gratifying. It resulted in lots of social contact that brought our two families together and gave me opportunity to meet his other children—my half siblings.' Monica paused for a moment and then continued

'My roots are what they are, and I'm glad I found Patsy and Charles. Meeting them has filled in some of the missing pieces in my self-understanding and we continue to relate well. Having said that, it is Pete and Olive who remain my Mum and Dad and that's who they will always be.' Though the earliest threads of Monica's life hardly promised to provide her with some of the finer fabrics of living patchwork, it was obvious she had gathered the best pieces available to fashion a life of personal fulfilment and profound joy. More than this, because of her community service, she had attracted the highest respect and esteem possible in the eyes of those who knew her. Her story makes me reflect and conclude that it is not how we begin life that matters so much, but what we make of it in the process of living.

I never did meet Monica's birth mother, but the lot of an Aboriginal woman has not always been easy. I came to understand this more fully when I began to lead a ministry for women throughout the South Pacific and met with groups of indigenous women in Australia. On occasion we would hold a weekend consultation to hear them describe their needs and to offer them support. I wanted to understand what they felt would help most, for these women were leaders within their own communities. As I listened I could hardly believe my ears. They spoke frankly of confronting drug abuse, alcoholism, incest and domestic violence present to an extent I could scarcely comprehend. These women had themselves grown up amidst such social ills, yet they were strong and stable with a keen eye to the welfare of their own people. Far from making excuses for deviant behaviour, they encouraged better decisions and improved lifestyles within their indigenous communities. They believed Aboriginals could make good choices and didn't have to sink to a low level. To the youth they had insisted,

'You're worth more. You're made of better stuff. You can make something of your lives—it's not impossible. If I could do it, so can you.' It was a powerful argument but one I couldn't use. They knew this, so they warned me, 'You won't be able to help our people directly because they won't listen to you. It's the tribal elders who have their ears. That means they'll listen to us because we're indigenous leaders. Thankfully, we can see benefit in what you have to offer so it's best if you resource us and we'll share with our people. That's the way they'll own the plan and be able to benefit from it.' I came away realising that cultural barriers stood tall between us, but I was yet to discover just how tall that was.

About a year later, mission headquarters drew up a new strategic plan for the South Pacific. The first initiative on the list was to foster increased literacy amongst the diverse peoples of the area and to include indigenous Australians.

'We've been doing that for island women for five years already,' I offered. This had come about because I had been introduced to Lois. She was the president of an organisation in the US that trained volunteers to teach literacy in developing regions of the world. With her help, we had set up training schools on a number of islands where literate women could learn how to teach others to read. 'The project was an unqualified success with hundreds of prospective teachers gathering to be trained in populated centres in Papua New Guinea and the Solomon Islands,' I effused. 'In turn, these women went out and taught thousands of other women from rural areas that were eager to know how to read.' With a smile that conveyed encouragement

Dr Bayles replied,

'Then you're the ideal person to lead a comprehensive literacy training program on our behalf and we will happily fund it.'

Conscious as I was of our Pacific island success and with the mission headquarters' mandate ringing in my ears, I set about developing a similar literacy project for Aboriginals living in a remote region of Western Australia. To run the program I needed an expert in the field and found Lance, a retired university lecturer with years of experience in teacher training and he volunteered to go. News of his coming spread quickly through the community and when he arrived he wasted no time in getting started.

On the first training day, curiosity brought several prospective students along. This promising group filed into class and sat gazing at the newcomer with dark deep-set eyes. In his verbal report on the experience, Lance recalled,

'The first day's instruction started uneventfully and the students seemed interested in learning. However, half-way through the morning there was a sudden commotion at the back of the room. The students had spied a large grey kangaroo bounding past the open window and they were agitated. My attention was also arrested by the animal's sudden appearance and, fascinated by its swift, graceful movement, I paused to watch it spring by and disappear over a sandy rise. When I turned to face the class again, the room was empty.' I stared at Lance in disbelief.

'What!' I gasped. 'Where had the students gone?'

'I wondered that too,' admitted Lance, 'but then I spotted them, spears in hand, disappearing over the same rise in hot pursuit of the kangaroo that would become the evening meal. It seems the sight of the kangaroo had stimulated their appetite for the hunt and their excitement didn't abate. There was no returning to the classroom that day nor any subsequent day either, I'm afraid. They'd given the program a two hour trial and judged it less interesting than other things. My attempts to gather them together to continue with the lessons proved futile. They simply never came to class again.'

Despite Lance's expertise the project ended in failure and I was embarrassed that we had wasted his time. Too late, I remembered the caution of the female community leaders and realised my mistake. Literacy had to be seen to be of value by the elders. Consultation at that level might take a long time but only if the elders saw light in a project, including literacy, would it be accepted by the people. Nonetheless, there is no doubt a successful literacy project was good for morale; mine included, for its success could be easily measured.

There were other aspects of ministry to all classes of women where effectiveness was not so easy to assess. This was because God, not man, was the main player. As I stood on a riverbank in Papua New Guinea one day, Esther was brought to me by a group of village women.

'Please pray for her,' they implored. 'When she goes home today, she'll be beaten by her husband.'

'How come?' I gulped.

'He doesn't allow her to come to any women's events but she came anyway,' they explained. I took Esther's careworn hands in mine and looked into her gentle, smiling face. Overwhelmed with a mixture of compassion for her and frustration that I could do little to help, I bowed my head and prayed for her protection. If I had misgivings about the outcome, Esther certainly did not. Like so many of her kind, she had a quality of faith scarcely known in my developed world. Often I had asked women like her if they thought we would be safe as we travelled in dangerous places. Always the answer was the same.

'Of course we will, we have prayed,' and that was final. I concluded that prayer was all they had and God knew it, so it was all they needed.

Another aspect of ministry with results hard to measure was the HIV/AIDS education initiative we launched and promoted all over Papua New Guinea. It was claimed that, thanks to the sexual irresponsibility of many itinerant truck drivers, the virus was out of control. Added to this was the ever-present cultural barrier that made the problem difficult to address. This was because discussion of any aspect of human sexuality was 'tambu,' meaning it was a forbidden topic and not to be broached by anyone. Here was evidence that though culture helps to define, it can also seriously limit. I concluded that the quickest way to gain cooperation on an issue was to work within a culture except when it impeded best outcomes. If it did impede, there would be slow, arduous progress towards cultural change and success would be doubtful.

Needless to say, there was no 'tambu' on asking for financial help from anyone who looked like they could give it. Once a woman in mid-life came alongside me and showed me her prosthetic leg.

'I got this one from the government, but it's so heavy,' she murmured. 'I would like one of those light ones but they cost so much and I haven't got the money.' The inference was obvious and similar requests abounded. There was a man who needed a wheelchair and another who wanted a zimmer-frame. A mother was looking for a sponsor to pay for her son's education. People in need were everywhere but one in particular claimed my attention.

'Come and see our school teacher, Maria. She's very sick,' invited Tess, a local leader.

'What's wrong with her? I ventured.

'She has cancer and would like you to pray for her,' was the straightforward reply. It is not a request I would refuse, so we set off for Maria's village. It was built of asbestos huts poised high above the water on the edge of a lagoon. Mounting a flight of wooden steps, four of us negotiated the rickety boardwalk that brought us to Maria's house. Narrower boards provided the fragile footpath that gave access to a fenced courtyard. This is where Maria lay on a low flat couch shaded from the heat of the sun by the shadow of her home. She smiled wanly as we approached and I was introduced. Soon we were seated on short-legged stools and Tess began to speak,

'Are you in pain today, Maria? We've come to pray for you.' Encouraged by her willing nod, I began a prayer I hoped would reflect Maria's needs. I asked for pain relief, for peace and comfort as well as strength for her family as they supported her. When we rose to leave, deep gratitude was evident in Maria's eyes while she whispered a quiet, 'Thank you.'

As we retreated over the same wobbly wooden slats that had brought us to Maria, I listened to Tess.

'It's going to be tough for the kids now that Maria can't work anymore. You see, they needed her wage to keep them in college. Her husband, Neil, doesn't earn enough to cover all their school expenses. They might have to drop out, or at least delay their training.' At that moment I heard my own voice speaking in my ear,

'This family has trouble enough with the imminent death of

the mother. They don't need to be under financial stress as well. You have the money to relieve them of this burden. Pay the college fees.' The debt was cleared while Maria still lived. After her death her family wrote me a tear-stained letter of grief and gratitude but the joy was mine to have been in the right place at the right time to help.

The next time I felt a similar urge was at a bus stop in rural Australia. I had come from visiting Mother in aged care in time to catch my usual bus. Soon, a young pregnant Melanesian woman with a three-year-old in tow joined me and we waited together. After some time it was obvious we had missed the bus. Whether this was because it had run ahead of schedule or been cancelled that day, we could not tell. All we knew was that it would mean a two hour long wait till the next one came. So we settled down in the bus shelter and fell to talking. I introduced myself and she replied,

'I'm Annette. My husband Aaron and I have come from Papua New Guinea so he can complete a degree in ministry. We were encouraged to come here by an Australian friend who said he would sponsor us,' she recalled.

'You mean your friend was going to pay your husband's fees as well as fund your living costs like rent, food and clothing?' I quizzed adding, 'How good it is to have such a generous friend!' At this Annette smiled and nodded her agreement.

'So how long have you been here?' I probed.

'Two years,' she replied.

'And has your sponsor been paying the bills?' At this she looked away for a moment and then returned her gaze to me and frankly responded,

'He has promised. We're just waiting for him to begin.' My next question addressed the obvious,

'So, how are you managing to live?'

'We both have jobs. Aaron works in a local food factory in the afternoons and I work at night cleaning offices. This pays our rent, our living expenses and fees for our girl at school. With a nervous laugh she added, 'I'm not sure what will happen once the twins are born.' Taken aback at the thought of twins, I retorted,

'I suppose there are still Aaron's tuition fees to pay as well.' At this Annette shrugged and confessed.

'We're living by faith and can only wait to see how God will work things out.'

At this point our conversation was interrupted by a clatter and a bang as a noisy rattletrap in the form of an old jalopy stopped on the road in front of us. From the open window, a longhaired man with a toothless grin greeted us. From his tattooed body, clad in a navy singlet, he waved a work-worn hand in our direction.

'Missed the bus, did yez?' he queried.

'I'm afraid so,' I admitted.

'It's an hour and a half till the next one comes you know,' he warned.

'Yes, we know they don't run very often around here,' I agreed.

'Where d'yez wan-a-go?' Taking hope from his question, I pressed,

'My friend here wants to get to the shops and I'm heading for the train station.'

'No problem, I'm goin' that way m'self. I'll take yez there.' Without hesitation we clambered aboard the dusty heap, grateful for the kindness of our rescuer. Moments later and sitting aboard the homebound train, the scene did not leave me: Annette's story of financial letdown; the goodness of the car driver despite his obvious limited means; and the sound of my own voice talking again in my ear.

'You have money enough to clear that tuition debt for Aaron. If you paid it into his account, you wouldn't even miss it.' A few discreet enquiries told me Aaron was stressed. He was falling behind in his studies and his grades were suffering. His tuition debt was growing and the arrears would prevent him from continuing until they were paid. Breach of the privacy laws notwithstanding, I asked a trusted friend who had access to student finances,

'By how much is Aaron's tuition in arrears?' After a moment's hesitation,

'$7,500 to date,' he replied

'If I were to send you a direct credit for that amount, would it clear his debt completely?' Assured it would, I made the transaction.

Next time I visited Mother, I told her of my missed bus and chance meeting with Annette. It was my mention of the two small children and the unexpected coming of the twins that touched her heart.

'How are they going to manage with four little children and no financial help?' she questioned. A week later I returned to find her beaming from her armchair.

'Here you are,' she exclaimed with characteristic candour. 'This is to help with the twins.' I took a white envelope from her hand and examined its contents. It contained ten $50 bills.

'Where did this come from Mum?' I asked in genuine surprise.

'After you left last week I started telling my friends here about the student family with two little children, twins on the way and no financial help. I said they need all kinds of baby supplies and clothing. Next thing I knew, they were coming to my room one by one and giving me $50 notes to help the parents manage.' Taking the cash, I deposited it anonymously into Aaron's account marked 'for the twins'. I knew the help was timely and came when it mattered most. With these opportunities came several welcome pieces to brighten my living patchwork, but not mine alone. Mother and her friends shared in the pleasure as well. Their lives were fraught with challenge enough as age delivered debility and decline, but in defiance of this, they looked beyond themselves and knew the joy of giving. This added extra beauty, perhaps in the form of a little trimming to a lifetime of living patchwork for them.

CHAPTER 19

To Live or not to Live

Sometimes there is little help for the needy when just a little help would be enough. I was sitting on the ground in New Guinea with a small group listening to island women tell their stories when a widow named Nina attracted my attention. She spoke of poverty and penury with a history of living from hand-to-mouth. Finding food to feed her family was a daily battle and she did not always win. One day in particular, she found herself penniless with no way to earn money and no means of buying food. In her distress she decided, for no special reason, to take the sandy track that led to the local market where an abundance of quality fruits and vegetables flourished on the stalls. Nina was walking barefoot with a simple prayer on her lips,

'Dear God, I must find food or my children will go hungry, please supply our need.' Scuffing her way along the path, she felt a buried object wedge itself between her toes. Thinking it might be a leaf from a nearby shrub, she bent to remove it. What she discovered was not a leaf but a folded five Kina note—enough to buy food for a whole day! To her mind, the absence of help from a human source meant God was his own aid agent.

When human help does come, it is clothed at times in comic dress. This is how it was in Fiji when four of us set off by car for an Indian Christian centre. We were forty-five minutes from the place when misfortune struck. A loud bang told us a tyre had blown out and the driver admitted we had no spare. Should more than fifteen minutes pass with no relief, we would be late and anxiety would grow amongst the waiting crowd. Knowing Fiji was as safe a country as any; I decided what to do and announced my plan to the others,

'I'm going to hitch a ride.' With that I opened a rear door and tumbled out of the car.

'I'm coming with you,' added Esiteri and we stood together on the side of the unsealed road—my arm extended and thumb pointed in the onward direction. In a matter of minutes, a large truck came hurtling along and, covering us in clouds of dust, pulled up sharply beside us. Grinning from ear to ear, two Fijian-Indian youths leaned out of the cabin window near us.

'Where do you want to go?' they asked. I explained our plight and they nodded,

'We know where the centre is. We can get you there in less than an hour,' they beamed and invited me to sit between them in the three seater cabin. With no other place for Esiteri, she scrambled up into the tipper body on the back of the truck and we continued on our way. The two young men said they were brothers and lived quite near our destination. During the conversation that followed, I learned their mother had been my fellow student in Australia some thirty years before and I relaxed in their cheery company. When they delivered us safely to the centre, we thanked them and exchanged smiles as they drove away with a farewell wave. It happened, we had arrived right on time, and so I turned to Esiteri to acknowledge our good fortune. Alas, the sight of her caused me to gasp in dismay. Her ride in the back of the truck had left her coated in black motor oil and a public appearance in that condition was out of the question. She was my local liaison officer, billed to make introductions and officiate at gatherings but she was decidedly indisposed and I had no option but to carry the day alone. Meanwhile, Esiteri spent the time at a backyard tap trying to scrub herself clean in cold water with no available soap!

They say, 'What goes around comes around' so a few weeks later, I was to find myself in Esiteri's shoes. I was now the liaison officer tasked with introducing Rhonda's successor, Dorothy, who was visiting from the United States. She had come to meet with large groups of women in the Solomon Islands and I was to officiate at the gatherings. We arrived on an island airstrip to find our only means of onward travel was by small outboard motorboat. As ill luck would have it, there was quite a swell on the ocean that day, so I sat on the outside nearest the water whilst Dorothy took her place in the middle of the craft. Fortunately, the tropical sea was warm, for the heavy spray splashed up over the side where I sat as we headed out to sea. As we ploughed through the waves, each successive surge raised a significant shower that made its mark until I was soaked to the skin. After an hour, we entered a reef and the water quickly calmed.

Soon the little bow nudged against a muddy bank that served as a primitive pier. With some help, we scrambled ashore and clambered up the slippery mud on all fours. Finally, we reached a grassy sward where we could stand up straight and stretch our aching limbs. It was then that I noticed Dorothy had not escaped the clutches of the swell and was nearly as wet as I was. I began to apologise for the irregular conditions we were facing, but she only laughed and said,

'Mine was a missionary family and I grew up in China through the 1950s. I know how to rough it.' That was enough for both of us and, dripping with sea water, we dissolved into peals of laughter.

While lighter moments brighten demanding days, there is no shortage of the darker times. One of these accompanied me to a primeval part of the Solomon Islands where I went on a special assignment to help with personnel problems. The place was undeveloped and isolated, full of challenge and with countless needs. Only the self-sacrificing from the developed world could survive there for very long. Soon after my return to Australia, the phone rang and I heard the familiar voice of Helen, a nurse I had known from chaplaincy days.

'My husband Stan's an accountant and we've been asked to go to the Solomon Islands to help with administration. It's just for a year,' she began. Helen had spent her childhood in Papua New Guinea, so island life was not new to her. 'I understand you've just come back from there. What kind of place is it? What were your impressions?' I thought for a moment before responding,

'It's raw mission life—very primitive and quite unsophisticated. As we arrived, the airstrip was swarming with people gathered for the weekly landing of the plane. Some of them were dressed like us while others came out of the jungle wearing pieces of tree bark or woven grasses. The men carried spears and machetes with the occasional local supi club. We were not in any danger though, for a delegation from the mission hospital met us and drove us to our accommodation. We stayed for three weeks and found the place and its people fascinating. There was so much from our culture that was unknown in the region and 'making do' became an art form for the expatriates living there,' I recalled. The voice on the phone continued,

'We have two girls and I'm wondering if it's suitable to take

them there. I have a few misgivings but I'm thinking it might offer them a unique experience for a year. If we do decide to go, they'd need to study by correspondence to keep up their schoolwork. Doing so, they'd be able to make a comfortable transition back to school when we return. They're good students so it shouldn't be a problem. Brittany will still be in primary school when we return but Tamara will be ready for high school.'
I pondered her query and replied,

'I think few kids would have an opportunity like this. It would be the experience of a lifetime for them.' Soon I was to eat those words and wish I had never uttered them. In due course, the family packed and left for the Solomon Islands, intent on offering some much needed service. What was unknown to any of us, however, was that some months before a white man had reprimanded a national in front of others for a perceived neglect of duty. The incident was seen as a public shaming by the locals and had not been forgotten. As a consequence, there would be reprisals.

Whatever their official role, missionaries tend to put their hand to whatever needs to be done and Stan was no exception. One day, about three months after his arrival, he had finished his office work for the day and had gone out to continue digging a partially finished trench destined to house drainage pipes. After bending to the task for a while, he straightened up to ease his back. At that moment, a well-aimed machete came slicing through the air. It had been thrown with expert precision and was intended to decapitate. The deadly weapon met its mark and Stan was swiftly beheaded. Horror and disbelief coursed through the compound. People were running this way and that in severe agitation while Helen and her girls were completely immobilised with shock.

Grief-stricken and sad beyond measure, Stan's family, reduced to three, forlornly gathered their possessions together and returned to Australia bereft. Thankfully, help and comfort awaited them, and once the funeral service had passed, they spent hours in counselling over several weeks. Back in the Solomon Islands there were court hearings for Helen to attend as the authorities tried to piece together the evidence and lay charges. Sadly, there was no satisfactory outcome. The murderer was protected by his own people and never did come to justice. Instead, it was left to Helen, Brittany and Tamara to create their own closure through faith and forgiveness. But, was this even possible? Apparently it was, for they did manage it. I observed in them neither bitterness nor hatred—only the same kind of strength and power to forgive that I had observed in Lindy Chamberlain when she was the victim of gross injustice, but that is another story.

Murder is not only prevalent in the Pacific islands. It happens everywhere, even in Australia. I was on my way to a church rally a good way north of Melbourne. The leader, Marilyn, was an Australian I had known from our time in California and she had briefed me on the expectations of the group.

'Come and tell us about your adventures in working with women in ministry,' she urged. 'To my mind, there probably isn't much new about it—just that it's been formalised and given a name. Haven't we women been ministering ever since time began? Still, it would be good for the men here to learn that the ministry of women is now recognised for what it is.'

An easy assignment, I thought. I am constantly talking on this topic. So, enthusiasm marked my acceptance,

'Sure, I'd love to do it and it would be great to see you again after so many years.'

The day before we were due to leave, a subdued Marilyn rang me again and her voice was strained,

'A terrible tragedy has befallen us. A dispute arose between one of our prominent farmers, George, and his next-door neighbour yesterday. At the height of the argument while tempers were hot, the neighbour fatally shot George and the community is devastated. We'd still like you to come, but please leave your women in ministry hat at home and bring us consolation in our grief instead.' I learned the murdered man had left behind his middle-aged widow, Betty, six children and an aged mother. I would spend the morning with the community at large and in the afternoon, I would visit the family. I knew they needed to talk, to tell individual stories of their relationship with George. I was aware of their unfamiliarity with me for I was a total stranger. Would they talk at all, or would we be locked in an awkward silence? Would they stifle their emotions and wait for me to leave before releasing their grief? I was tempted to avoid the visit, pleading privacy on their behalf, as I reluctantly walked towards their front door.

Regardless of my fears, a warm welcome greeted me; the children hovering near while Betty began to speak.

'It doesn't seem real. George has, I mean had, a strong assertive personality and was clearly the head of our house. I keep expecting him to come in through the door, and for everything to continue as usual. I can't believe he's gone.' At this, her tears began to flow and the children drew closer in solidarity with their mother. 'I can't believe he's gone,' she sobbed. This was the phrase that would linger in my mind after years of hearing it on the lips of so many grieving people. A woman named Joan said it when her friend Phil suggested they each move on from the loss of their partners to start a new life together. An ageing Pat said it when visions of the past loomed more real than a picture of the present. Hesitant Gloria said it when her children tried to convince her that a move to a smaller, more manageable home would be worth considering. With my eyes still focused on Betty, I continued to listen.

'Will I ever get over this?' she whispered. Her experience was so fresh, her feelings so raw that no assurances of recovery that I could offer would mean much. Nonetheless, I could say,

'It won't always hurt like this. It will get better. Just as the body heals, so does the heart when it is broken.'

'I'll never forget him, you know,' she wept.

'Of course you won't. He'll always remain a very big part of your life,' I comforted. Remembering George did remain important to Betty and though she healed from grief, the years they had spent together and the children they had produced held indelible memories for her. Her life with him was like a long chapter in a book she was continually writing. As the weeks and months passed by, she realised the chapter entitled 'George' had drawn to a close. New people and experiences no longer shared with George were the substance of the next chapter. Some years later when the last of her children had left home, Betty remarried and began yet another chapter continuing to write her story of living patchwork.

Life is fragile at the best of times but in the case of one baby girl named April, it was especially so. There was consternation in my daughter-in-law Elaine's voice as I listened to her on the phone.

'My youngest sister, Polly, recently gave birth to a little girl and at first the baby seemed to thrive. After two weeks, however,

Polly was worried. Some serious signs began to appear in April and she was airlifted to the premier paediatric hospital. It has emerged that she has a grossly underdeveloped heart and is not expected to survive. There simply isn't enough tissue for the organ to function. The specialist team says she has little or no chance of coming through this. Polly and her husband, Clem, think they may well lose her.' As I listened to Elaine, a strong urge within me said,

'Pray,' and I replied, 'We will pray. No one else can help, only God.' I knew Polly was a believer and would put her faith in God. So with no time to lose, I began to call on the many men and women I knew who would join me to pray. Mother gathered a group of residents and staff in her aged care home to pray and I met with 300 fellow believers in church to lead them in a prayer of healing for baby April. I am not normally given to sensation nor to seeking impressions but as I lifted my voice to God that morning, a deep peace descended on me with the calm assurance we had been heard.

Soon I was on the phone to Elaine once again,

'How is baby April?' I asked, hoping to be heartened at her reply.

'It was looking pretty hopeless at one point, but there's been a marked improvement. The doctors are amazed and there's some indication she might pull through after all.' I came away with a song in my heart for I could only praise God. April continued to gather strength and to develop normally. Today, all there is to show for her ordeal and the close brush she had with death is a scar resembling a small zip fastener in the middle of her chest where the surgeons had tried to help. God's intervention was not lost on Polly.

'I knew the odds were against our baby's survival,' she

reflected. 'Somehow God, in his great wisdom, saw fit to answer the prayer of faith in her favour. Thank you so much for what you did.' My friend Denise heard April's story and crafted a splendid little quilt in a crazy patchwork design. Along the bottom in applique she added the word: 'Casting all your care upon Him, for He cares for you.' As she makes her way through life, not all April's patches will be splendid, but this one certainly was.

For the encouragement they bring, such stories as I have told are worth the telling. Undoubtedly, they uplift the hearer as they inspire the writer. If they are to endure as part of living patchwork in the lives they represent and find matching moments in the experience of many more, they must be written down and made accessible. The medium for this is the printed page or its counterpart; the electronic version. As it is, encouragement is a two-way street for it was with encouragement that I began to write these chapters in the hope that my words may be a means of encouraging others.

CHAPTER 20

To Write or not to Write

'You ought to write.' It was said to me more than once and especially after I had taken a talk that was thought to be worthwhile. Indeed, I had written. There was more than a score of articles, several stories, some poems, a set of study guides and even a weekly self-help series that had run as a column in a monthly magazine for more than a year. Two forewords bore my signature and I had even written a book that featured long forgotten female figures. They were wives and daughters of men of high profile whose stories had never been told. The book was no novel, but contained accounts of real women with lives of courage beyond common fear, self-development over self-indulgence and self-sacrifice above self-interest. Yet, the editor I thought might publish it sounded sceptical,

'Those kinds of books are out of favour,' he judged. People don't read them anymore. Readers are not impressed with the notion of a faultless hero with a perfect past. The lives of your wonderful women are too far out of reach for the average. Nowadays, a kind of iconoclasm prevails where readers identify better with flawed individuals. It's the 'warts and all' sort of truth that sells today. As far as sales go, self-help publications do much better.' Since he had roundly rejected my book, I decided for the first time in my life to self-publish. Happily, I was at an advantage with marketing. Like featured speakers before me, wherever I travelled to address a sizeable audience, I took care to use the opportunity to promote the book. Because of this, demand soon outstripped supply and I sold every copy in print.

Perhaps this success in acceptance and sales went to my head, for I began to think again about the suggestion John had made to me to write a PhD thesis. Soon, the idea no longer seemed foreign and even started to feel familiar. Eventually, it became a task sitting on my 'to do' list and I took it for granted I would attempt it. When John had stood beside me at his graduation holding his newly acquired degree, his face had worn a thoughtful expression. Then he had turned to me and said,

'Thank you Honey, for your practical help and consistent support. Without your cooperation, I wouldn't have achieved this goal. Now, with my help and support, it'll be your turn to earn a doctorate. There's no question you have the ability.' Alongside these words from decades past, gentle nudges from other sources continued to push me towards the task. One came from Shaun, a former work colleague who enthused,

'I'm about to start formal study for a PhD. I've developed an interest in nineteenth century religious history and am told a terminal degree will lend credibility to the books I'm already writing on the subject.' Another came from a female pastor who met me for a chat about her ministry. In the course of our conversation she said,

'I've begun research for a PhD in biblical studies,' and I was impressed. A second woman in ministry came apologising,

'I'm so sorry for pulling back from full-time ministry. I'm sure it must be a disappointment to you but I need to make some space in my schedule for doctoral studies.'

'Excellent choice,' I assured her. 'It's the right time of life for you to do it.' Old as I was, there was no doubt I felt a tug towards academic action by these conversations and they helped lead me to a firm decision. A question still remained, however. Would I have Leo's support? I knew I could only do the work if he was in favour of it, for its greatest impact would be on our daily lives. When I shared the notion with him, his reply was predictable,

'Great idea—why not?—go for it! I will support you all I can.' At that point neither he nor I knew just how much this would entail. In the future he was destined to read and re-read lengthy sections of material I had written with themes unfamiliar to him. He would hunt down typographical errors and question punctuation. His regular routines would be significantly interrupted as they gave way to my deadlines. He would be called on to transport me to a number of academic events and, at times, be left to cook his own meals.

Assured of Leo's support, my next step was to visit my Australian alma mater where, forty eight years before, I had earned a lowly certificate. In the meantime, the college had become a university with the right to confer degrees including PhDs. Fortunately, there would be no delay in starting, for the bachelor's and master's degrees I had earned in the United States had equipped me to enrol immediately in a doctoral program. Yet, I hesitated for one issue could have deterred me from undertaking the heavy study load and that was my severely limited vision. Still, accessibility to more and more electronic material that could be enlarged on my oversized computer screen to any extent I needed saved the day and made the project possible.

There followed an interview with a prospective supervisor named Jim, and it went better than I could have wished. In the working relationship we were destined to develop, we casually adopted first names and our regular progress sessions were easy and relaxed. Jim was a semi-retired, seasoned scholar with lots of knowledge and enough time to liberally dedicate to my work. He had a kindly mien and a stronger belief in my potential to succeed than I had. His support throughout the four years it took to complete the degree was invaluable.

In the early days I craved more specific direction than Jim tended to offer and as time went on, I began to see that we are always at our cleverest when aided by hindsight. I could have wished for this gift at the outset. Had I possessed it, I would have seen more readily the folly of embarking on the project with no clear notion of a topic. Jim was of the opinion that this did not matter because writing a PhD includes,

'Running down blind allies and finding dead ends until you discover the way you really want to go.' This sounded like an exercise in frustration and a waste of time to me, but Jim's strength was in developing expansive ideas that multiplied options and he was very good at it. Finally, it was one of his ideas that grabbed my attention and I decided to test it. I had already settled on a theme as my focus area from the biblical book of Acts when Jim casually commented,

'Have you noticed the frequent mention of body parts in Acts?'

'Sounds rather forensic,' I quipped. 'What should I do with body parts?'

'You could think about them,' was his enigmatic response. On my way home I asked myself the question,

'What do people do with body parts?' The answer startled me as it flashed across my mind, 'Of course, people communicate nonverbally with body parts!' Immediately I had my topic and it was new and untouched in the field of New Testament studies.

I determined that the effectiveness of nonverbal communication could only be evaluated by its results and not by its practice. In this way I could avoid cultural contamination in any attempt to derive its meaning. I went about assessing results in the use of hands and feet by the disciples of Jesus as they communicated his message. The research took me from two stories about healing in Acts to Luke's other book, his Gospel, and from there to the version of the Bible most accessible to him—the Greek translation of the Old Testament. Rather than English translations, my studies depended on ancient Greek texts and included Jewish writings available in the first century of our era, nor was that all. Because of the prevalence of healings in Acts, I also researched the writings of ancient Greek medical authors and traced the origins of quotations cited in Acts from Classical Greek literary sources. All was in an attempt to pin down the effectiveness of the kind of communication in focus.

The work took me on virtual visits to archaeological museums in Russia, continental Western Europe and the United Kingdom. These housed ancient Greek artworks like painted vases depicting plays and terracotta votive offerings to the gods. Amongst these, I found no lack of illustrations of active human body parts including hands and feet. There was also no question my living patchwork was taking on fresh vitality as I worked in the vibrant environment of new discovery.

The stuff of living patchwork can quickly pale and fade, however, with the arrival of a nasty shock. Though my colleague Shaun and I had worked together on our early research methods, we had gone in different directions for the substance of our study. This meant it had been several weeks since we were in contact when I met his sister-in-law, Paula, in a grocery store,

'Have you heard about Shaun?' she enquired.

'Heard what?' I probed.

'He had a skin lesion frozen with liquid nitrogen but it turned out to be melanoma. It has spread through his system and he's having chemotherapy.' At the time a melanoma diagnosis was a virtual death sentence and I feared for Shaun's future. Blessed with a sanguine personality, he optimistically believed a cure would be developed soon, so he continued to work on his research. Tragically, in just a few months, he developed secondary brain tumours and it became hard for him to think. Eventually, having lost his vision and his mobility, he was admitted to a hospice where I visited him in a private room. Bending low with my ear to his lips, I heard him whisper,

'I'm not sure I'll be able to finish my thesis.' Defeat had never been in Shaun's sights for any project he had undertaken, so I knew these words were more than hard for him to voice. He smiled weakly at my unrealistic attempt to defuse the seriousness of the moment,

'It might be hard for you to get down the aisle Shaun, so I'll be marching for both of us and we'll share the degree,' I affirmed. His words had been the first sign of resignation I had seen in him and the last I was to hear him speak.

Shaun's family called on me to organise his funeral and I stood with them at his graveside to watch his coffin sink irretrievably into the ground. At that moment, my thoughts centred on the futility of death. There had been such high hopes for Shaun and now there were so many shattered plans. Even more sobering was the knowledge that, out of the two of us, the one in the lowered coffin could easily have been me. Then I considered Shaun's legacy, his organisational ability that had seen me swept up and included in his plans to present historical papers. I remembered his invitations to lecture to seminarians on the art of preaching to women and the times he had favoured me as the main speaker for an event. I recalled the respect he had extended to me in comments free from gender bias. In all these ways he enabled me to serve without restriction and according to my God-given strengths.

But, Shaun's disease and death were not limited to someone else's misfortune. Indeed, they came perilously close to my own life. I was halfway through the task of writing when I made a routine visit for a medical check to Margaret, my local GP. I had sensed nothing out of the ordinary except for a small sticky mucous discharge that I thought hardly worth mentioning. I hesitated in Margaret's presence, in two minds as to whether I should bring it up or not. Then, on my way out, I finally decided to include a comment about it,

'It's probably not worth raising,' I apologised.

'Anything odd is worth raising,' she countered and ushered me back towards the examination table. I left her office equipped with an order for an ultrasound,

'Just to make sure everything's OK,' she smiled. At the imaging centre the technician was not convinced everything was OK. He seemed to take a long time stroking over the same abdominal spot with his smooth-topped probe and I ventured,

'What are you seeing?'

'There's something on top of your bladder. You'll need to go back to your doctor about it.' Back in Margaret's office once more, we discussed the next step and she offered,

'There are several urologists in our area. Let's choose one

for you to see.' Soon Leo and I were meeting with Dr Chan and he was showing us images of a tumour sitting like a top hat on the dome of my bladder,

'We'll need to remove this. It's a minor procedure. We can approach it internally so there'll be no incision. We'll give you an appointment for early next week and you'll only be in hospital overnight,' he advised. With plenty of hope for a quick solution to a small annoyance, I was admitted for an overnight stay. The morning after, a rather grave Dr Chan stood at the foot of my bed and explained,

'There was more to the tumour than I anticipated. I know I didn't get it all. It'll require major surgery with the removal of your bladder and the attachment of an external bag. When the pathology results come back telling us what kind of tumour it is, we'll make a date for surgery.' With that he went, leaving me reeling from the news and its implications. I had some friends with urostomy pouches and in the ensuing days I cried on more than one shoulder at the prospect of joining them,

'You get used to it and it isn't so bad,' said one.

'I have no trouble with it, it's easy to manage,' assured another. Three weeks elapsed before Leo and I were back in a pre-operative consultation with Dr Chan,

'The pathology results show a rare, aggressive cancer. It's not a common bladder tumour but a urachal adenocarcinoma.' Leo nodded, but I had no idea what this meant. As though reading my thoughts Dr Chan continued, 'It will still mean major surgery but the good news is we will be able to conserve your bladder.'

'What will the surgery entail?' asked Leo.

'We'll remove the urachus and umbilicus where the cancer originated as well as the top third of the bladder. Over time the bladder will stretch to its normal capacity. Because it's so rare, little is known about this cancer. Apart from surgery no effective treatments have been developed. There is no chemotherapy at present and it doesn't respond to radiotherapy. Consequently, the survival rate is poor and catching it early gives you the best chance. We will also take some lymph nodes from the abdomen to test for any spread of the malignancy. As laparoscopic surgery is my specialty, this is the method I will use.'

Sobered to the point of silence, Leo and I left Dr Chan and headed for home. Gradually, I began to share my diagnosis with family and friends. The same people who had prayed so fervently for little April now gathered to pray for me. Those who had undergone major surgery, for whatever cause, called to share their concern and common experience. They were fellow travellers on the journey of life who came from unexpected places and we walked together as they offered me their understanding. The one chance I had was that the cancer might not have spread and the imminent extensive surgery would remove it all.

Concern was etched on Leo's handsome face as I left him and disappeared down the hospital hall to the surgical waiting room. Once I was dressed in a gown and cap, a fatherly wardsman wheeled me towards the operating theatre. He parked my trolley in a small anteroom and, patting my foot through the blanket, departed with the ominous words, 'I wish you well.'

'Well' may have described the ultimate outcome but not the process. The operation took three hours with another three in recovery. The days that followed passed in a blur of pain and discomfort while I waited impatiently to fully heal. In the meantime, good news came with the report that there was no evidence the disease had spread. Encouraged by this and propped up on cushions in my office chair, I continued to write my thesis. I was thankful beyond measure that, short of following Shaun to the cemetery, I could fulfil my promise to him to walk down the aisle at graduation and receive my PhD. Symbolically, it would be for both of us.

While cancer may have been a common affliction in the developed world, it was HIV/AIDS that ravaged developing countries with cruel indiscrimination. During its increase to epidemic proportions in Africa, my friend Gerard fell into conversation with me at a social event. Having grown up and lived in South Africa until his mid-forties he was well acquainted with conditions on the continent of his birth,

'I've just returned from a work assignment in Kenya,' he began. I knew of his expertise in IT and assumed this had been his reason for going there.

'Interesting?' I casually enquired. His reply was rather intense and it surprised me,

'Always interesting…but tragic.' Curiosity aroused, I leaned in to hear what he meant,

'I came across an unusual village in a remote region about two hours from Nairobi. It had been established by a group of widows with their children. Their husbands had all died from AIDS and some of the women were sick too. I discovered the widows had fled into the bush to escape the local custom of remarriage to a relative who had two or three wives already. Hard though it was, these women preferred to fend for themselves. For housing they had built some natural bush shelters but had no means of support beyond a little garden plot. As long as it rained enough they could grow a few vegetables but basically, they were very poor.

They're desperately in need of help and…' At that point our conversation was interrupted and never to be continued, but I remembered it.

Some years later I phoned Gerard's grieving widow, Penny. In the wake of his recent death she was clearly worried about the future of his African AIDS project and how it would be funded now that he was gone. She confessed her incapacity to fundraise and lamented,

'I'll try, but I'm so bad at it!' A clear recollection of my unfinished conversation with Gerard flooded my memory and, this time, a wave of compassion engulfed me. I felt for Penny in her recent loss and for the burden of care for the African project that had become hers. I felt for the widows and orphans in their suffering and destitution too, and realised there was money, and to spare, that would ease their rugged plight,

'I'll get you some money, Penny,' I soothed with no idea of just how. Apart from soliciting coins by shaking a tin with a slot in its top out on the public footpath, or going door-to-door collecting for a needy cause, I had never done any serious fundraising. At my words, gratitude bubbled out of the phone and I knew the promise must be kept.

It was not hard at first to raise a few thousand dollars with a series of talks at dinners and lunches, but then I had a windfall. I mentioned the project to Charlie, who listened and came back with a suggestion,

'I think I have an answer, Mum,' he declared. 'I have lots of contacts in the musical world, young up-coming performers of promise. How about I organise a Christmas concert where the performers donate their talent? We could charge a moderate entry fee and the proceeds would support Penny's Africa project.' As a result, Charlie's concert became an annual event raising more than $50,000 in all. Consequently, the project was able to buy its own land for a market garden, to build an all-purpose commercial centre and to buy a marquee with chairs that could be offered for hire. Inevitably, the life of the original widows was shortened by AIDS and when they died their orphaned children were cared for by the others in African village style. The death of a widow left room for a newcomer with her children. As a result, the number of widows remained the same while the number of children grew. Despite ongoing health struggles, the widows managed to become self-supporting to a degree, while other donated funds built them a school and paid a teacher's wage. Over the years several of the children grew to be educated adults and employed contributors to the needs of the village that had raised them.

If lending a little help to Africa was my focus, it was a beckoning hand from Mongolia that waved to Leo. Wesley, a friend in retirement, felt urged to go to the capital, Ulaanbaatar, where there were serious medical needs and few resources. He phoned Leo and invited us to accompany him. Leo was to lecture on health and I was to speak on human relationships. Our group numbered about fifteen with some IT specialists and a nutritionist as well as teachers of English as a second language. We arrived in late summer when sleet was already beginning to fall with the promise of a harsh winter to come.

As part of our healthy living initiative, we had thought to introduce the people to a wholesome vegetarian diet. One of our first assignments was to make an inspection of the grocery stores to see what fresh foods were available. We had to smile at our naivety because there was no green vegetable in sight. The only plant food on sale was an array of shrivelled root vegetables that had seen better days. Clearly, the population lived mostly on meat eaten with a fermented mare's milk drink. After a few days in the country most of us had succumbed to a local flu-like virus complete with hacking cough and raging headache that lasted a week or more. Added to this was the language gulf—an obvious barrier to forging friendships with the people. Communication was only possible through a translator who was not always available. It was tempting to feel resentful when the fine rice paper pages of some of the Bibles we had distributed for free, were used to roll cigarettes. Nevertheless, there were many grateful people who owned that our visit had brought a life-change for the better for them. Though the Mongolian visit could never be called a tourist trip, we did take a day or two to travel into the steppe country. Our route took us past clusters of tent-like yurts to wide expansive grasslands. Groups of nomadic horsemen rode across these open plains, straight backed and bearing Saker falcons perched on their protected arms. The men were driving herds of shaggy yaks, whose wild flower flavoured milk was recommended as a delicacy. In the evening, throat singers entertained us accompanied by the haunting strains of the traditional horsehead fiddle—a type of long-necked lute.

To my mind, tourism may ensure a sanitised glimpse of the new and the novel, and it may be enough for some. For those who have the chance, however, it is in living with the people that really reveals their story. I wished I could claim that experience in several parts of the world but then I would need more than one lifetime to do it. As it is, living patchwork brought me much to cherish and some to regret. Wanted or not, the pieces I have are mine and they must be included to make an authentic whole though the pattern be truly crazy.

Epilogue

It is late autumn, and relative to the seasons of life I am getting on. Last month David and Charlie sponsored a grand celebration for my eightieth birthday and I am still revelling in its afterglow. This week Mother's Day brought me an enormous bouquet of English roses and Asian lilies to remind me once again of the love of my sons. Charmed by their thoughtfulness, I walk from room to room breathing in the perfume of the exotic blooms. Soon, ninety-one year old Leo will finish mowing the lawns and join me for morning tea when we will sit on our shaded patio and overlook the sparkling pool. As usual, the sun is shining in full splendour from a cloudless sky on our private piece of paradise; our back garden. Today there is birdsong on the air floating down from the leafy trees clustered all about us, though the volume and variety is less than in spring. Just now, the fairy wren, willy wagtail and noisy miner have disappeared to leave the pied currawong and common magpie warbling in harmony with the rich melody of their sinister cousin, the butcherbird. Busily scratching in the soft earth, the peevish plover and foraging turkey make an untidy pair as they scatter the mulch beneath a lilly pilly shrub. Overhead, the cacophony of a morning kookaburra choir has ceased and given way to the piercing screech of a flock of cockatoos, come to raid our berries and nuts. Living as we do on an ocean inlet, the occasional ibis or heron drops in to pay us a call whilst a baggy beaked pelican saunters past our gate with all the time in the world at its disposal. Early today, wild ducks perched atop our slanted roof bent on settling on the swimming pool at the first opportunity. It is only Leo's diligence that keeps them at bay and allows statuesque 'Harry', our resident water dragon to sun his slender body undisturbed beside the streaming waterfall.

As it happens, Harry and I share a similar passion for water. Though he enjoys lying near it, I am content to immerse myself in it. This means that a lap-pool and spa are important inclusions in the design of our retirement home. For exercise, forty laps in the heated comfort of the clear water and a soak in the warmer spa have enduring appeal. When the season turns and cooler weather comes, I reluctantly forsake the pool to walk a five kilometre trek each day with a neighbourhood friend.

When Leo and I are not travelling, the rest of my day is spent preparing presentations, writing pieces for publication and entertaining guests because I love to cook. I love to cook but not to sew. Despite the gift of a sewing machine from my father and the enthusiasm of my daughters-in-law for the art, sewing of any kind has never been a skill of mine. I can only covet the ability of family and friends when I see the beautiful work they produce but I cannot emulate it. Visually ill-equipped as I am, I do not have the capacity to do it well. I recognised this inability early when my first sewing teacher examined my work and bluntly declared,

'Oh dear, your hemming is like a row of cat's teeth. Can't you do it a bit more neatly than this?' Having no close contact with cats, I was unfamiliar with the shape of their teeth and wondered why the comparison. At the first opportunity, I examined the teeth of my Aunt Ivy's cat and discovered the likeness was apt, for feline teeth were anything but even. Furthermore, I knew neat sewing would always be beyond me and a sewing machine would not help. So, when it came to completing the patchwork quilt of long ago I had to face these facts. The quilt was real enough and destined to be beautiful if crafted by hands other than mine, but with words coming to my aid it was better for me to transform it into a metaphor and allow it to illustrate circumstances, experiences, and choices in life. I felt a patchwork metaphor was well-suited to this purpose and creating it fell within the limits of my ability.

Now the question remains; what ever became of the literal quilt; did it serve a useful purpose or was it discarded? Though I lacked the skill to make the quilt, I retained the 'thrift' ethic that had inspired it in the first place. Mortified at the thought of wasting it,

I had turned to Mother for advice.

'You've got pluck for even attempting to make it,' she affirmed. How about you take it to our dressmaker, Mrs Magee and get her to fix it up. After all, she did rescue your sewing assignment for school last year and I'm sure she'll be able to do the same with this. Don't worry about the cost. She can add it to the account I have with her and your Father will pay.' This sounded like a good solution and I grabbed it. Due to domestic violence, Mrs Magee had fled her home to become a single mother with three children to support. Fortunately, she had a gift for dressmaking. Her work was of the highest quality and her fees were low. Mum wanted to support Mrs Magee so she sent as much work as she could her way. At Christmas, Dad made sure the Magee children had treats to eat and presents to open. The youngest, Violet, came away on camping holidays with us and took to calling my kind-hearted father, 'Daddy.'

Over the next two weeks Mrs Magee painstakingly unpicked my sewing disaster and made a beautiful padded cover of my patchwork quilt. When it was finished I could barely believe its perfection. Every line was straight; each patch fitted its place precisely and the mismatched textures and tones presented a pleasing crazy pattern. On the day of the competition, with some trepidation, I proudly submitted my entry to the judges.

'Did you make this all by yourself?' they marvelled. I had not wanted to lie but the temptation to impress was too great.

'Yes,' I nodded, claiming credit where no credit was due. Scepticism swept over the faces of the judges as they pressed,

'Are you sure you made it all by yourself?' Clearly, I was not believed; nor did I win the prize. I had not deserved to win, but ultimately, the day taught me a salutary lesson in integrity.

With respect to moral development, I was witness to a fair degree of expediency during my formative years. This amounted to taking the easy option in order to gain a desired end. It allowed for deception, falsehood, theft and broken promises. Of those closest to me, it was Mother, who set a clearer moral course even though her advice about using the skills of Mrs Magee was questionable,

'If you want people to respect you, you need to be honest, trustworthy and responsible. Nobody looks up to someone who lies and cheats,' she avowed. Her words hit home and I began to value personal integrity and to look for it in other people. Along with the rest of humanity, I knew how good it felt to be respected and how bad it felt when respect was lost.

'Respect is based on community values and expectations,' said my mentor Veronica. 'When you live up to these, you gain respect. When you keep living up to them, you retain it.'

'What if you aren't consistent in this?' I queried.

'Occasional lapses may be overlooked if they are not thought to be too serious but if you keep disappointing the community, it lowers its expectation of you and you lose some of its respect.'

'What if no one but you knows you have failed to live up to community values? I protested.

'If your personal ethics reflect the values of the community, and you violate them, you'll suffer a loss of self-respect, even if no one else knows about it.' I wondered if there were other elements alongside personal ethics that attracted respect. Could it be generated by good performance or even a fine appearance? Veronica was decisive,

'That depends on the values of the community. A sporting club will admire and affirm on the basis of performance and a glamour group on the basis of appearance. By and large, however, it is character that attracts the greatest community respect. It is also character that lies at the foundation of self-respect.'

'I suppose you're going to tell me that universal values like honesty, integrity, trustworthiness and responsibility are the building blocks of character?'

'...nothing less than these, in fact. The point, of course, is that living by these values also affects self-esteem and can ultimately determine self-worth.'

As I considered this, I recognised that despite my best efforts, there was often a gap between my values and my behaviour so I challenged Veronica,

'This makes anyone who honestly wants to uphold their values, a hypocrite because nobody really does it; at least, not perfectly.'

As I meditate on this problem, I think again about Mrs Magee. In order to create a beautiful patchwork quilt, did I not take my tangled effort to her for help and had she not transformed it into a piece of perfect workmanship? It was obvious that though the quilt was mine, all credit was due to her for its transformation. My character is mine also and despite the circumstances, experiences and some choices that affect it, damage it or mar its potential beauty, I can take it to my Maker for he promises to transform character. This process of transformation takes time; is tortuous and will not be completed in a lifetime. There is good news, however, for while I wait for him to finish the transformation, Jesus replaces my damaged character with his own and in God's eyes I am already complete.

From the patchwork metaphor I have learned that living patchwork in a world of mixed and misplaced pieces delivered by circumstance, experience and sometimes choice can, in retrospect, produce a thing of beauty after all. From the literal quilt I have learned that nothing I try to create is ever perfect, especially not my own character, but God is able to make me whole regardless, and I just continue to trust him with every aspect of my life.